Leading Pharmaceutical Innovation

Springer
Berlin
Heidelberg
New York
Hong Kong
London
Milan
Paris
Tokyo

Oliver Gassmann · Gerrit Reepmeyer
Maximilian von Zedtwitz

Leading Pharmaceutical Innovation

Trends and Drivers for Growth
in the Pharmaceutical Industry

With 53 Figures and 20 Tables

 Springer

Professor Dr. Oliver Gassmann
Gerrit Reepmeyer

University of St. Gallen
Institute of Technology Management
Unterstrasse 22
9000 St. Gallen
Switzerland
oliver.gassmann@unisg.ch
gerrit.reepmeyer@unisg.ch
www.item.unisg.ch

Professor Dr. Maximilian von Zedtwitz

Tsinghua University
School of Economics and Management
100084 Beijing
People's Republic of China
zedtwitz@em.tsinghua.edu.cn

previously with IMD-International,
Lausanne, Switzerland
permanent e-mail:
max@post.harvard.edu
www.technomanagement.net

ISBN 3-540-40717-0 Springer-Verlag Berlin Heidelberg New York

Cataloging-in-Publication Data applied for
A catalog record for this book is available from the Library of Congress.
Bibliographic information published by Die Deutsche Bibliothek
Die Deutsche Bibliothek lists this publication in the Deutsche Nationalbibliografie; detailed bibliographic
data is available in the Internet at <http://dnb.ddb.de>.

Springer-Verlag is a part of Springer Science+Business Media

springeronline.com

© Springer-Verlag Berlin · Heidelberg 2004
Printed in Germany

Softcover-Design: Erich Kirchner, Heidelberg

SPIN 10952153   42/3130-5 4 3 2 1 0 – Printed on acid-free paper

Preface

Pharmaceutical innovation is like gambling at roulette, only the stakes are higher. Considerably higher, since the most recent estimates put the costs of drug development at US$ 800 million to US$ 1 billion – per drug! This is equivalent to the price tag of the Empire State Building, when it was for sale a few years ago. In 2001, the major US and European pharmaceutical companies invested more than US$ 30 billion in R&D, at a higher R&D-to-sales ratio than virtually any other industry, including chemicals, automobiles, electronics, aerospace, and computers.

Delivering a blockbuster drug is the Holy Grail for any pharmaceutical company. But in the last decade the rules of developing blockbusters seem to have changed. On the one hand, more sophisticated screening technologies, genetic engineering, and expanding networks with biotechnology companies increase the probability of commercial success. Critical success factors include the discovery phase and a stronger outside-in orientation in the early innovation phase. After the implosion of the high-tech stock market, biotechnology and other technology-driven opportunities may have lost some of their attractiveness for big pharma: a pipeline of solid and predictable innovations seems to be the highest goal of most pharmaceutical companies again. On the other hand, despite significant investments in pipeline management and novel technologies, there is still no recipe for ensuring a blockbuster hit. Instead, a disturbingly large number of blockbuster drugs were actually a result of serendipitous discoveries and unplanned spill-overs, such as the discovery of Viagra during blood-pressure related research. Despite decades of intensive research, we are still far away from being able to predict and measure the efficacy of pharmaceutical R&D.

So, is it 'back-to-basics' then? The three simplest but perhaps most difficult challenges that increase R&D productivity in pharmaceutical innovation are:

- Increasing the number of new and commercially successful products;
- Decreasing R&D and lifecycle costs;
- Decreasing development time.

'You can't manage what you can't measure', so goes an old managerial saying. In this book we are trying to develop a case for the manageability of pharmaceutical innovation despite its apparent lack of measurability. We understand pharmaceutical R&D management as vertically integrated activity which is not restricted to top management. As many scientists in research and almost all scientists in development are also managers, we would like to address them in their double roles of managerial decision makers and scientists.

Based on extensive research on innovation and R&D management in multinationals in several industries, we started to focus on the pharmaceutical industry in order to identify some key drivers and mechanisms of pharmaceutical R&D. Over the past years, but in particular in 2002 and 2003, we interviewed senior R&D and general managers of pharmaceutical companies around the world. We also did a fair share of background research such as studying intelligence reports, press releases, articles, publications, company presentations and searching the Internet. In second-round meetings we tested our hypotheses and theories, and we sharpened our examples and insights for managing R&D in the pharmaceutical industry. In addition, we conducted a workshop with 14 selected international experts on pharmaceutical R&D, during which we identified and consolidated new and emerging trends in pharmaceutical innovation.

We concentrated on Swiss pharmaceuticals for two reasons: Firstly, we had gathered substantial insight in the Swiss industry sector over the last few years while based at the University of St. Gallen and the Institute for Management Development in Lausanne. Swiss pharmaceutical companies were thus convenient yet also extremely telling examples. In fact, one chapter of this book was written around a study entitled 'Managing R&D in the Pharmaceutical Industry: The Case of Switzerland', which had been conducted for and financed by the Yokohama National University and the Health Care Science Institute in Tokyo (see also a Japanese translation of the report in the Journal of Health Care and Society, vol. 13, no. 2).

But more importantly, Switzerland assumes a unique role in pharmaceuticals worldwide. Nowhere else is the pharmaceutical industry's relative importance for the national economy as high as in Switzerland (in terms of contribution to GDP, see page 23), and Swiss life science companies represent a surprisingly wide spectrum of the worldwide pharmaceutical and biotechnology industry within a relatively focused geographic area. We thus illustrate many of our findings with examples from the Swiss pharmaceutical industry. Also, we present two short case studies of the two largest Swiss pharmaceutical companies, Novartis and Hoffmann-La Roche, as an appendix to this book.

Few other industries are as driven by science, research and development as are pharmaceuticals. We therefore placed a deliberate emphasis on issues related to research and development within the wider realm of innovation. However, we also looked at other central areas of pharmaceutical innovation, such as the management of human resources, project and portfolio management and outsourcing. Moreover, the increasing importance of globalization in pharmaceutical science, technology and product development is covered in detail. This is also reflected in three core chapters of this book which are directly based on three key areas from which pharmaceutical companies expect major innovative developments to enhance innovation and productivity of pharmaceutical R&D:

- Novel R&D technologies, such as high-throughput screening and gene splicing;
- Reorganization and fine-tuning of R&D pipeline management;
- Outsourcing and internationalization of major phases of the R&D process, including basic research, candidate identification, and clinical development coordination.

These three themes are introduced in chapters 3, 4, and 5. Chapter 6 illustrates how some of the key management problems are dealt with by industry. We summarize our insights in a concluding chapter on perspectives and trends in pharmaceutical R&D and show some future directions for managing innovation in the pharmaceutical industry.

This book would not have been possible without the encouraging support of our research interviewees in various companies and their dedication to make sure that we understood the issues correctly. They spent valuable time sharing their thoughts and knowledge. In particular, we would like to thank Dr. Goetz Baumann, Marc Boivin, Jeff Butler, Dr. Gunter Festel, Dr. Urs Hofmeier, Dr. Marc Müller, Dr. Pius Renner, and Dr. Philipp Steiner. We are also grateful to Dr. Werner Müller of Springer for managing the overall publication process smoothly. Writing this book has been a great learning experience for us, and we hope the leading principles and examples of how to best manage pharmaceutical innovation included here are equally useful and inspiring to pharmaceutical managers and students of the pharmaceutical industry alike.

St. Gallen, Lausanne, Beijing   Oliver Gassmann
                                        Gerrit Reepmeyer
October 2003   Maximilian von Zedtwitz

Contents

I. Innovation as a Key Success Factor in the Pharmaceutical Industry

„Pharmaceuticals are the most cost-effective, value-added, least-invasive part of the healthcare system. "

Alan F. Holmer,
President of Pharmaceutical Research and Manufacturers of America (PhRMA), 1998

The Productivity Paradox

Despite its high R&D intensity, the pharmaceutical industry is facing an increasingly dire situation. On average, only 1 out of 10'000 substances becomes a marketable product. And only 3 out of 10 drugs generate revenues that meet or exceed average R&D costs (see Reuters 2002).

By definition, R&D productivity is the ratio of input in R&D versus its output. The black-box in between consists of the drug development pipeline, new screening and research technologies, worldwide cooperation networks in clinical research and testing, and a whole new armada of licensing and cooperation agreements with competitors and biotechnology start-ups. Still, as a recent Reuters study (2003a) shows, R&D performance of the major pharmaceutical companies is sub-optimal:

- Pipeline output is low and declining;
- Costs of R&D are rising rapidly, driven by larger and more complex clinical studies and expensive new enabling technologies;
- Over-supply of 'me-too' launches and a lack of genuinely innovative drugs make it difficult to replace revenues lost through patent expiry;
- Protracted clinical trials and administrative procedures reduce the marketed shelf life of patented products.

R&D expenditures account for a large share of the overall cost structure in the pharmaceutical industry. As the effective cost structure of an original product may vary considerably from case to case, generalizations about fixed percentage levels for the various cost factors cannot be made. Hence, the following table cites ranges rather than exact figures. A large proportion of the margin is reinvested in new drug R&D.

Table 1. Average cost structure of a newly developed drug.

Relative Contribution	Cost Factors
20% - 40%	Research, Development, Licenses
15% - 30%	Production
5% - 15%	Technical and Administrative Costs
20% - 30%	Marketing and Distribution
20% - 35%	Margin

Source: Pharma Information (2002)

In addition, R&D expenditures of the pharmaceutical companies worldwide have grown constantly over the last decades (in relative terms, from 11.4% of sales in 1970 to 18.5% in 2001), and according to PhRMA (2001), the major US and European companies invested more than US$ 30 billion in 2001. But in the 1990s, the launch of new molecular entities on the market has declined or has been constant at best (Fig. 1). The number of new drugs approved by the Food and Drug Administration (FDA) in the United States fell to just 15 in 2002. This is less than half of the annual average over the previous years.

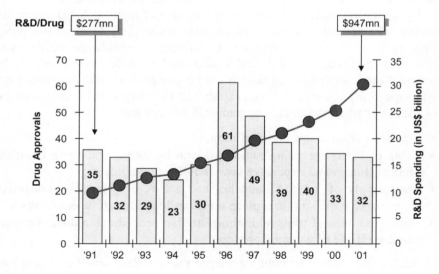

Source: PhRMA (2001)

Fig. 1. The productivity gap in the drug discovery process.

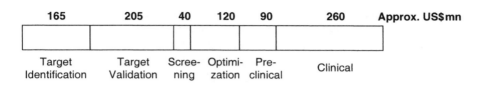

165	205	40	120	90	260	Approx. US$mn
Target Identification	Target Validation	Scree-ning	Optimi-zation	Pre-clinical	Clinical	

Source: BCG (2001)

Fig. 2. Breakdown of drug R&D expenditures. Cost to drug includes failures; target identification includes activities outsourced to academic research institutions.

Consequently, drug development costs per new drug approval are constantly increasing. In 1976 it cost US$ 54 million to develop a new drug, US$ 231 million in 1987, and about US$ 280 million in 1991 (DiMasi 2001). This number has grown to close to US$ 1 billion by now (see Fig. 2 for a detailed breakdown of R&D expenditures). Even though it is not legitimate to make a direct comparison between R&D spending and R&D productivity, the tendency of increasing R&D costs per drug is certainly a concern with top management in pharmaceutical companies.

The situation is particularly precarious for big pharmaceutical compa-

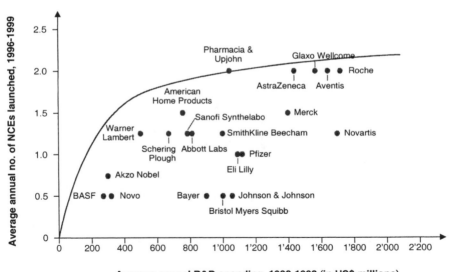

Source: KPMG (2002) based on Lehman Brothers estimates

Fig. 3. R&D productivity as a number of launched, new chemical entities.

nies. R&D productivity as number of launched new chemical entities (NCEs) is very low for most of the major companies (Fig. 3). According to research by KPMG and Lehman Brothers (2002), Roche and Novartis spent on average about US$ 1.7 billion in R&D per year from 1992 until 1998, but launched on average just 2 or 1.2 new chemical entities per year between 1996 and 1999, respectively.

Furthermore, the average duration of drug development has increased since the 1960s, although it seems to have leveled off in the 1990s. Modest time gains seem to have been made mostly during the drug approval stage (i.e., after most R&D has actually been completed) and where the cooperation and involvement of regulatory authorities is paramount. The average time a drug candidate spends in clinical trials, however, has increased since the mid-1960s, from 2.8 years to 6.6 years by the 1990s (Fig. 4).

In summary, pharmaceutical innovation at the beginning of the 21st century is faced with the following challenges:

- Increasing R&D costs;
- Declining per-drug productivity;
- Long development times;
- Growth of generics.

A significant increase in productivity in pharmaceutical innovation is needed in order to close this widening productivity gap and to meet reve-

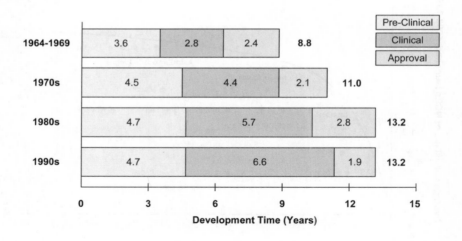

Source: Pfizer (1999)

Fig. 4. Time spent by a drug candidate in the pre-clinical, clinical and approval phases.

nue growth expectations of 5% to 10% per year. This seems like a tall order, given that most mature industries have not grown by more than 1-2% over the past years. Only the fastest growing market in the world, China, has grown by more than 8% in the same period.

In the pharmaceutical industry, however, worldwide sales have grown at an average annual rate of 11.1% from 1970 until 2002 (PhRMA 2003). Today, these double-digit growth rates are strictly incorporated into the industry's overall growth expectations. As success raises stakeholders' expectations of further success, pharmaceutical companies are forced primarily by investors and management to at least maintain this growth rate for the foreseeable future. The winners in the pharmaceutical industry even have to exceed these growth expectations in order to deliver above-average returns to their shareholders. For the past decades, the silver bullet for achieving these growth rates has been the blockbuster.

The Blockbuster Imperative

Reliance on blockbuster drugs – a drug with at least US$ 1 billion in annual sales – has remained a largely unquestioned growth strategy of most leading pharmaceutical companies, and is often quoted as the only viable way to meet the high growth expectations. One reason is that blockbuster drugs offer relatively high returns compared to lower value drugs, due to the substantial risks, time and costs involved in product development and commercialization. In addition, developing drugs with blockbuster potential is a more sustainable growth strategy than relying on patent defense.

In 2002, 58 ethical pharmaceutical products have been considered blockbuster drugs. Cumulatively, they represented more than US$ 120 billion in sales, the equivalent of approximately one-third of the global pharmaceutical market (Reuters 2003a).

However, problems experienced by companies like Merck and Schering-Plough, both of which are/have been heavily reliant on blockbuster revenues but are now faced with patent expiration and maturing drug portfolios, raise the question of whether blockbusters can or should remain a focus of future growth. Analysis conducted by Reuters (2003a) during the first half of 2002 shows that 15 out of the 44 blockbusters in 2000 had lost or were due to lose US patent protection before the end of 2002, exposing approximately US$ 30 billion of revenues to generic competition.

Furthermore, looking forward, the blockbuster market in 2008 will be worth only 1.4 times that of the blockbuster market in 2000. Thus, companies can no longer rely on these products to drive double-digit revenue

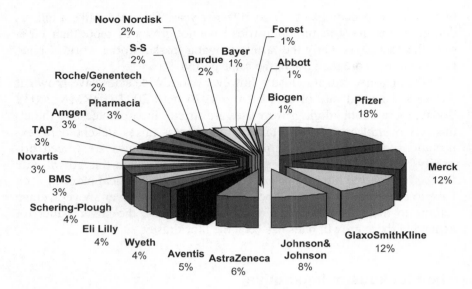

Source: Reuters (2003a)

Fig. 5. Share of the global blockbuster market by company in 2002.

growth. A company generating US$ 30 billion of revenues in 2000 must increase its sales by an additional US$ 23 billion by 2008 if its investors' 10%+ annual revenue growth expectations are to be achieved. Therefore, a US$ 1 billion product in 2000 will need to be a US$ 1.8 billion product in 2008. While in the first half of 2002, 53 products with the potential to generate annual sales of US$ 1 billion or more in 2008 were identified, only 21 of these were considered to have the ability to exceed US$ 1.8 billion (Reuters 2003a). Thus, the requirements of blockbuster products – to reach almost US$ 2 billion in annual sales – will be increasingly hard to accomplish in the future.

In 2002, 24 companies were responsible for marketing the 58 blockbuster drugs. The most successful company was Pfizer owning about 18% of the worldwide blockbuster market (see Fig. 5).

However, with individual company blockbuster sales ranging from just over US$ 1 billion to more than US$ 22 billion, and blockbuster growth rates varying from -28% to more than 45%, there are clearly considerable variations in the dynamics of the blockbuster market (Fig. 6). In this blockbuster comparison, Pfizer tops the list as the most successful company with blockbuster sales of more than US$ 22 billion and a blockbuster sales growth rate of about 20% between 2001 and 2002. Merck and GlaxoSmithKline with about US$ 15 billion in blockbuster sales come in second

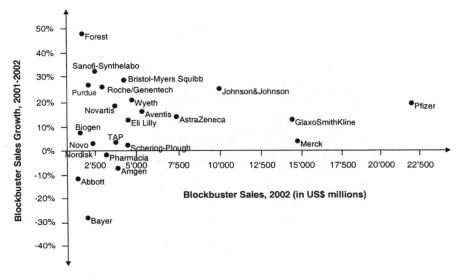

Source: Reuters (2003a)

Fig. 6. Blockbuster sales and sales growth by company from 2001-2002.

and third. Bayer, however, owns just one blockbuster product and reported a significantly negative blockbuster sales growth.

The 10 best selling blockbuster products including their indication, marketing company and therapy area are listed in the following table.

Table 2. Global blockbuster products in 2002.

Rank	Brand	Indication	Marketing Company	Sales [*]	Therapy Area
1	Lipitor	Dyslipidemia	Pfizer	7'972	CV
2	Zocor	Dyslipidemia	Merck	6'200	CV
3	Losec	Ulcers	AstraZeneca	4'623	GI
4	Procrit, Eprex	Anemia	J&J	4'269	Adjunct
5	Norvasc	Hypertension	Pfizer	3'846	CV
6	Zyprexa	Schizophrenia	Eli Lilly	3'688	CNS
7	Prevacid	Ulcers	TAP	3'600	GI
8	Paxil, Seroxat	Depression	GlaxoSmithKline	3'304	CNS
9	Celebrex	Arthritis, pain	Pharmacia	3'050	Arth. pain
10	Zoloft	Depression	Pfizer	2'742	CNS

* in US$ million

Abbr.: CV cardiovascular; *GI* gastrointestinal; *CNS* central nervous system

Source: Reuters (2003a)

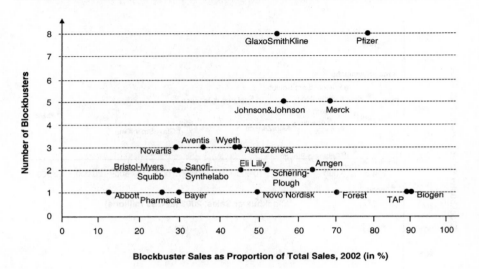

Source: Reuters (2003a)

Fig. 7. Contribution of blockbuster sales to ethical sales in 2002.

Only two companies – GlaxoSmithKline and Pfizer – own eight block-buster products. The majority of companies owns between one and three blockbusters (see Fig. 7). Companies, such as Pfizer, Merck, Biogen, or TAP, depend very much on their blockbuster products. Blockbusters were responsible for the majority of ethical sales by contributing between 70% and 90% to total revenues. Firms with a more diversified product portfolio include, for example, Abbott, Bayer or Novartis.

Today's blockbuster market is dominated by cardiovascular and central nervous system (CNS) therapies (Fig. 8). In fact, with combined sales of more than US$ 57 billion in 2002, they represent nearly half of all block-buster sales (i.e., 27% and 21% respectively). Other major therapy areas of today's blockbuster products include gastrointestinal (9%), respiratory (9%), infectious disease (8%), and adjunct therapy (7%).

Underpinning blockbuster success in the cardiovascular and CNS markets is a substantial patient population and a high degree of unmet need. More than 300 million people in the seven major national markets (US, UK, Japan, France, Germany, Italy, Spain) suffer from the most common form of dyslipidemia, hypercholesterolemia, making it one of the most prevalent conditions in the Western world (Reuters 2003a).

Three of the top five cardiovascular blockbusters are anti-dyslipidemics; Pfizer's Lipitor (atorvastatin), Merck's Zocor (simvastatin), and Bristol-Myers Squibb's Pravachol (pravastatin). Backed by intensive marketing

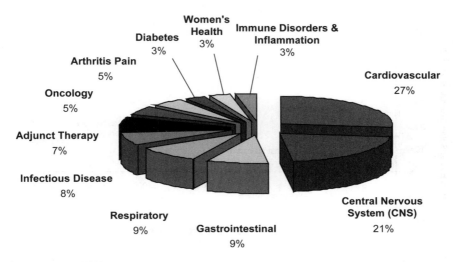

Source: Reuters (2003a)

Fig. 8. Segmentation of the global blockbuster market by therapy area in 2002.

support from Pfizer, Lipitor has become the most lucrative pharmaceutical product of all time.

Sales growth of cardiovascular and CNS blockbusters has been driven primarily by the increasing success of existing rather than new blockbusters, although a small number of products enjoyed their first year as blockbuster drugs in 2002, including Johnson&Johnson's pain patch, Duragesic (fentanyl), and Novartis' anti-hypertensive, Lotensin/Lotrel (benazepril).

According to their respective growth potential, the therapeutic areas of the blockbuster market can be differentiated between stable and emerging blockbusters (see Table 3).

Table 3. Classification of therapeutic areas and blockbuster markets according to Reuters.

Stable Blockbuster Markets	Emerging Blockbuster Markets
Gastrointestinal	Adjunct therapy
Respiratory	Oncology
Infectious disease	Arthritis pain
Women's health	Diabetes
	Immune disorders & inflammation

Source: Reuters (2003a)

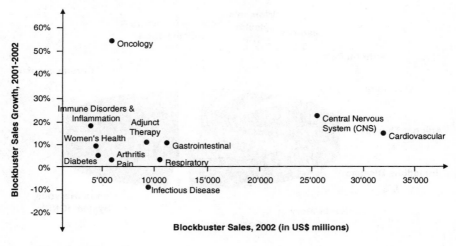

Source: Reuters (2003a)

Fig. 9. Blockbuster sales and growth by therapy area from 2001-2002.

Stable markets are already served by highly effective drugs that treat large patient populations. Their levels of unmet therapeutic need are typically lower than in the cardiovascular and CNS areas, resulting in lower blockbuster growth rates. Sectors classified as emerging blockbuster markets are characterized by a high level of unmet therapeutic need. In general, their growth is being driven by the introduction of selective products that offer high efficacy and response rates.

Reflecting respective market sizes, the therapeutic areas can be classified according to their overall market attractiveness as measured by their blockbuster potential (Fig. 9).

Strategies for Growth

Where does growth in the pharmaceutical market come from? According to an IMS Health (2000) study, drug spending increased by 18.8% in 1999. The lion's share (10.8%) is derived from increased utilization, 4.2% is accounted for by price inflation, and only 3.8% comes from truly new medicines, that is pharmaceutical innovation.

Usage, prices, and applications of drugs are influenced by a great number of stakeholders in the pharmaceutical industry, as we will see below. While overall healthcare costs are increasing, a series of studies by Lichtenberg (1996, 2000) showed that increased spending on prescription drugs actually leads to overall decreases in healthcare spending. He found that a reduction of US$ 71 in non-drug spending was accompanied by an US$ 18 increase in newer prescription drugs, resulting in a net savings of US$ 53.

Prices are typically strongly regulated by the state. Because of the critical situation of the healthcare sectors in most developed countries, we have seen administrators use a blanket approach to curb healthcare costs, ignoring the potentially compensating effects of new drug use as described by Lichtenberg (2000). Additionally, growth from new applications and customers has limited potential in saturated markets and markets with low purchasing power such as developing countries. Pharmaceutical innovation and the number of new products will have to increase in order to sustain growth.

From a company's perspective, growth in market share can also be achieved externally: Many pharmaceutical companies have made headlines because of recent merger & acquisition (M&A) activity. The most recent examples of large mergers include Pfizer & Pharmacia, Ciba & Sandoz, and Astra & Zeneca. Still, the industry has further M&A potential and is far from consolidation: The top 10 pharmaceutical companies in aggregation have less than 50% market share (see Table 4).

Table 4. Largest pharmaceutical companies in the world in 2001.

Rank	Company	Country	Revenues [*]	Market Share [in %]
1	Pfizer	USA	26.3	7.5
2	GlaxoSmithKline	UK	24.6	7.0
3	Merck	USA	18.6	5.3
4	AstraZeneca	UK	16.1	4.6
5	Johnson&Johnson	USA	15.6	4.4
6	Bristol-Myers Squibb	USA	15.0	4.3
7	Novartis	CH	14.1	4.0
8	Aventis	F	12.2	3.5
9	Pharmacia	USA	11.9	3.4
10	Abbott	USA	10.8	3.1
11	American Home	USA	10.7	3.1
12	Eli Lilly	USA	10.2	2.9
13	Roche	CH	9.7	2.8
14	Schering	USA	8.3	2.4
15	Takeda	JP	6.3	1.8

* in US$ billion at manufacturers' prices; prescription drugs

Source: Pharma Information (2002)

Why do companies merge? One of the most frequently offered reasons for mergers is the exploitation of synergy effects, resulting in the reduction of costs in administration, sales, and development. Another reason is the access to new markets and industry subsectors. Thus, it is claimed that 'added value can be generated for investors'.

Mega-mergers do not necessarily result in higher market share or greater productivity, as illustrated by a recent study by Wood Mackenzie (2003). Grouping the top 10 pharmaceutical companies in 'mega-merged companies' (Pfizer, GSK, BMS, Aventis, Novartis, Pharmacia) and 'non-mega-merged companies' (Merck, J&J, Eli Lilly, Roche), they found that between 1995 and 2002, 'mega-merged companies' lost on average 2.8% of their worldwide share in the ethical drug market, while 'non-mega-merged companies' won 10%. They also found that 'mega-merged companies' appear to produce fewer NCEs after their mergers than before (see Fig. 10).

Why do mergers remain attractive? Pharmaceutical companies pursue a mix of defensive and aggressive growth strategies. Defensive strategies aim to retain a competitive position by means of co-marketing agreements, co-selling, cross-licensing, and market-related acquisitions among others. This strategy builds critical size and momentum, reduces costs of sales, and essentially creates entry barriers for newcomers (see also chapter 2). Aggressive strategies try to overcome entry barriers set up by competitors: companies develop and apply new technologies, complex knowledge and project portfolio management (the pipeline), pursue outsourcing and inter-

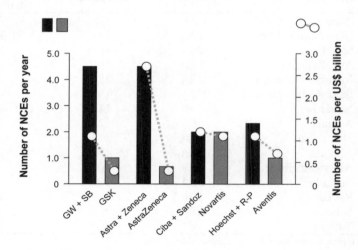

Source: Wood Mackenzie (2003)

Fig. 10. R&D productivity (measured in NCEs decreased in top 10 pharmaceutical companies) 3 years before and 3 years after the merger.

nationalization. While this strategy does not immediately reduce overall costs, it does provide a greater potential for creating value-added and hence long-term cost reduction.

Some companies pursue a balanced strategy of both approaches, whereas others seem to have made a choice. In this book, we focus more on the latter type of strategies.

Do You Want to Be in This Industry?

„Longer term, I am convinced that societies will see the special value and benefit of pharmaceutical innovation. We'll be a healthy, vibrant industry for the future. "

Fred Hassan,
then CEO at Pharmacia, 2002

Along with the product groups of vitamins, fine chemicals, plant protection agents and animal medicine, pharmaceuticals belong to the broader category of so-called life science products (i.e., products that intervene in the metabolic processes of living organisms). Including specialty chemicals, the different product categories of the pharmaceutical-chemical industry are characterized as follows:

- The pharmaceuticals product group includes mainly patented, innovative products available only by prescription. Recently, over-the-counter (OTC) drugs and diagnostic aids have increased in importance.
- The product group of plant protection agents includes herbicides, fungicides and insecticides. The animal medicines group includes drugs for pets and livestock.
- The vitamins and fine chemicals product group includes the 13 vitamins and their derivatives as well as flavors and fragrances. These are not products for direct consumption, but rather 'bulk products' that are used for manufacturing pharmaceuticals, foodstuffs and animal feed.

The specialty chemicals product group comprises of a number of highly specialized products that are frequently manufactured in relatively small quantities in response to specific needs of individual customers. With these products, professional advice to customers is a rule of considerable importance.

How attractive is the pharmaceutical industry overall? This question cannot be adequately answered without addressing the balance of power among the various industry stakeholders. In addition, the exit barriers of existing competitors and the entry barriers of potential new companies have to be analyzed. Is the pharmaceutical business a profitable one to be in? Given the high return-on-equity ratios (around 27% in mid-2003) and net profit margins (around 21% in mid-2003) of pharmaceutical companies, one might suppose that the industry is characterized by little competition and safe and predictable environments.

A method that is often used to analyze industry attractiveness and identify opportunities and threats is Michael Porter's five-forces framework (Porter 1985; see Fig. 11). Porter summarized five principal forces that shape competition in an industry: the bargaining power of suppliers and buyers, the risk of entry from potential competitors, the threats of substitute products, and the degree of rivalry among established companies within an industry. In the pharmaceutical industry, we have identified the regulative force as the sixth element of competition. Several opportunities

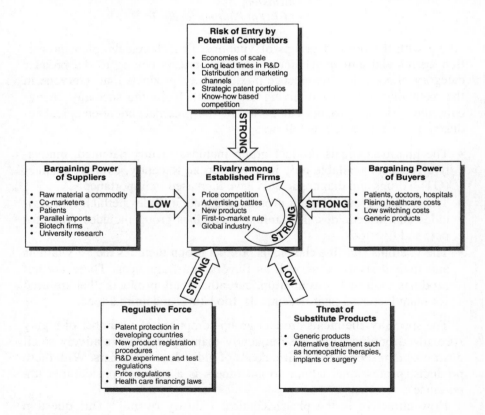

Fig. 11. The balance of power in the pharmaceutical industry.

and threats of the pharmaceutical players directly derive from public regulations.

Bargaining Power of Suppliers

Suppliers in the pharmaceutical industry include providers of raw materials, biotechnology firms, and manufacturing plants, but also local co-marketing partners or the labor force. Pharmaceutical companies may have different suppliers if they compete in the OTC, ethical or generic businesses.

In the pharmaceutical industry, suppliers do not seem to have strong bargaining power. In clinical research, for instance, the suppliers are patients who participate in clinical trials, the investigators and their research teams who provide the data, and external contractors. An additional threat may emerge from parallel imports from low-price countries (which has triggered heated discussions over the prospects and dangers of adapting prices for life-saving but expensive treatments to developing economies and the possible threat of re-imports from these countries). However, pharmaceutical companies are increasingly dependent on small biotechnology companies and university research. Since the biotechnology venture capital industry has matured in the past years, it has become more difficult to acquire biotechnology start-ups (although some biotechnology companies have started to aggregate and announce their intention to become fully-fledged pharmaceutical companies, e.g., Celera and Axys Pharmaceuticals in 2002). Alliances have thus become an important source of new products and marketing agreements.

Bargaining Power of Buyers

> „We must never forget that innovation is an access issue – access for those with unmet medical needs. We must balance the needs of patients for marketed medicines today with the needs of patients depending on new medicines in the future."
>
> Henry A. McKinnell, Jr.,
> President and CEO, Pfizer, 2002

The buyers are patients (particularly in the OTC business), medical doctors who prescribe drugs, hospital boards who authorize the purchase of new treatments and drugs, pharmacists optimizing their stock of medication, etc. Buyers of pharmaceutical products are still a highly fragmented group, but pharmaceutical companies have been successful at establishing direct marketing relationships with doctors and patients. Buyers can exercise a strong influence over prices, often seeking price reductions for bulk purchases or threatening to switch to other suppliers (particularly in the generics business).

The buying power of doctors seems to have increased, and switching costs are low. At the same time, governments and health authorities influence local prices in their attempts to contain healthcare costs. In countries with nationalized healthcare and tight prize controls, buyer power is higher: Prescription prices in most European countries are about 30-50% lower than in the US (Freudenheim, Peterson 2001).

Risk of Entry from Potential Competitors

New entrants are usually faced with the following entry barriers:

- Economies of scale such as in R&D, marketing, and sales;
- Slow success rates in new drug development;
- Image, established relationships, and brand value;
- Capital requirements and financial resources;
- Access to distribution channels;
- Ability and capacity to deal with regulatory agencies and patents.

Even small biotech firms focusing on a single technology must spend hundreds of million of dollars just to propose a potential product. Established pharmaceutical companies have manufacturing and distribution systems that are hard to replicate, a strategic patent portfolio preventing competitors to enter new disease areas, and large marketing budgets to protect their brands. Nevertheless, some companies are trying to enter the pharmaceutical market, such as contract research organizations vertically expanding their businesses.

Furthermore, patent protection does not protect against competition from generic products. However, while generics capture about 50% of unit sales with continuous growth, they are far less profitable. Pfizer's 2001 prescription drug revenues of US$ 26.3 billion was almost five times the combined sales of the 11 leading generic drug makers covered in Standard & Poor's Industry Survey (Saftlas 2001).

Threat of Substitute Products

Substitute products perform the same function as existing products, or better. Generic products are serious substitutes for original products at a lower price. They mount an increasing threat to profitability of large pharmaceutical companies. However, they might also offer opportunities. Novartis, for instance, proactively approached the threat of generics and now has emerged as the largest generics company in the world by selling various generic products under the global umbrella name Sandoz.

Certain medical devices, alternative therapies, or hospitalization may be substitutes for drug treatments. For instance, surgery may make drug intervention unnecessary. On a cost-to-value basis, however, surgery, prolonged medical care and hospitalization are less attractive.

Alternative therapies such as homeopathic remedies, acupuncture, and herbal medicines are all still considered medically unproven and are usually not covered by health insurance. But traditional treatment knowledge might change with a new generation of medical doctors who are educated more openly and are trained to consider the certain patients' wish for soft treatments. If these products begin to demonstrate medical efficacy, they will be quickly absorbed to become part of conventional medicine. Overall, thus, the risk of unmanageable exposure to substitute products in the pharmaceutical industry is relatively low. Strongest product substitutes still come from the innovative pharmaceutical companies themselves.

Regulative Forces

Public laws and regulations play perhaps a greater role in the pharmaceutical industry than in any other. The regulative force impacts pharmaceutical innovation on several levels: (1) R&D regulations and product registrations, (2) price regulations and national healthcare systems, and (3) intellectual property rights.

R&D regulations in experiments are mainly affected by national product registration agencies, such as the Food and Drug Administration (FDA) in the US or Swissmedic in Switzerland. These governmental agencies stipulate authorization and registration procedures for all new drugs submitted for approval in their respective markets. Animal trials and inventions in gene technology are covered by strict authorization processes as well. New drugs must prove that they are suitable for use in human beings and the respective benefit-risk profile has to be determined prior to marketing approval. Only after a medicinal product has cleared all hurdles –

and therefore fulfills regulations regarding quality, efficacy, and safety – is it granted authorization. An accelerated approval may be granted to priority drugs that show promise in the treatment of serious and life-threatening diseases for which there is no adequate therapy. For example, when the first tests of the antiviral drug AZT in 1985 showed encouraging results in 330 AIDS patients, the FDA authorized a treatment referred to as 'Investigational New Drug' for more than 4'000 people with AIDS before AZT was approved for marketing.

In most countries prices are regulated by federal authorities (directly or indirectly). In some countries the price of a product is fixed according to the social costs of the society. Yet in other countries, the price of a drug is defined by its innovativeness as measured by the number of patents in that area (e.g., Brazil). However, national healthcare systems always have the primary and most direct impact on product prices, which are reimbursed by health insurance organizations.

The overall purpose of patent law is to support research and ensure that all interests are satisfied. On the one hand, innovations should be made available in the interest of the public. On the other hand, innovators should have an incentive to innovate by being assured that their inventions are protected against unlawful imitation and replication of their knowledge. From a competitive perspective, patents are essential because it is not difficult to ascertain the respective substances of a drug and, consequently copy or imitate pharmaceutical products. Studies have shown that patents are the most effective means of appropriation. 65% of pharmaceutical inventions would not have been introduced without patent protection, compared to a cross-industry average of 8% (Reuters 2002). Patent protection is unclear in some key areas of pharmaceutical R&D, for instance at the time of writing it is still unclear to what extent genes can be patented (and thus 'owned'). Sometimes, international patent law is only accepted if national interests are maintained. Brazil, for example, threatened over the last ten years several times to suspend domestic compliance with international patent rights for malaria drugs unless certain license fees were dropped.

Rivalry among Established Companies

The rivalry is moderately intense since the pharmaceutical industry is still comparatively fragmented. Although the top 10 drug manufacturers control about half of the market, no single company controls more than an 8% share. Competitors try to improve their position in the marketplace by means of price competition, acquisitions, advertising battles and new product introductions. This rivalry is particularly intense in saturated markets (e.g., pain relievers), and less intense in growing markets (e.g., AIDS).

Most industry profits come from patented products or therapies, 'me-too' products tend to be less profitable. As individual drug therapies tend to be quite focused on particular markets, competition is somewhat limited. Nevertheless, generics are improving their position at the expense of blockbuster drugs going off patent (experiencing price drops of up to 80%), and have increased their share of unit volume to 47% in 2000, up from 33% in 1990 (PhRMA 2001).

Rivalry is typically fought over time-to-market, since first-to-market companies gain a relatively high market share and thus are more likely to recoup R&D and marketing expenses. Global product introductions help achieve market share, and therefore large companies have an edge over smaller companies thanks to more developed marketing and distribution systems.

Differentiation via Clinical Profiles

A drug's clinical profile influences its commercial success. In general, a product's clinical profile consists of four major criteria (see Reuters 2003a):

- Efficacy;
- Safety/side effects;
- Dosage/administration;
- Costs.

In other words, if a product is efficacious, has negligible side effects and can be administered with a convenient dosing mechanism, it is in a good position to compete in most markets. The degree to which a product can be differentiated by any or all of these criteria varies by therapeutic market and competitive environment. For example, late market entrants offering only marginal improvements in efficacy may need to enhance their commercial prospects by competing on the basis of a lower price. Alternatively, trials can be designed to target areas of unmet need, for example efficacy in specific patient subpopulations or improved dosage schedules.

Clinical trial data are typically generated during the drug's development in the clinical phases I to III. As the pressure for product differentiation has significantly increased in the pharmaceutical industry, it is increasingly common for companies to conduct phase IV trials after a product has been launched. Such trials typically focus on further indications and subpopulations or seek to differentiate a product from its major competitors through head-to-head studies. Once valuable trial data has been generated, it is important to convey the information to key audiences, particularly opinion leaders and high prescribing physicians, in such a way that a product's benefits relative to its competitors are clear.

Entering the Market Quickly

Factors that influence a product's market penetration are greatest from five years prior to about one year after the product launch. The growth rate and market share gained in the first year after launch largely determine overall sales that can subsequently be achieved (Reuters 2003a). Consequently, this period attracts the majority of promotional resources relative to any other year in the lifecycle.

Just like any other product, the typical drug lifecycle can be broken down into three major phases: growth, maturity and decline. Accordingly, the growth phase offers pharmaceutical companies the greatest opportunities to influence their revenue prospects. Numerous products, including blockbusters like Pfizer's Lipitor and the former Pharmacia's Celebrex, illustrate this pattern. All of these products experienced above average sales growth in their first year on the market and have since continued to display strong sales performances. Although there are cases where first year market performance was good but sales did not meet long-term expectations, this is usually due to a major external event, for example the discovery of major negative side-effects.

The market dynamics during the product launch are determined by three closely-linked determinants. To improve the probability of a new drug becoming a blockbuster, the product should be (see Reuters 2003a):

• Early to enter a particular therapy area or product class;
• Positioned relative to existing competition;
• Accompanied by heightened pre-launch awareness.

Notably, pre-launch promotion has become more important in recent years. A new product's rate of acceptance can be significantly boosted if the market is well prepared for it. The key focus of such investments is raising awareness among physicians and, eventually, patients. This is particularly important in new areas when a product is first to market or if there is little awareness of the disease, its symptoms and treatment options.

Marketing departments are working increasingly close with their R&D counterparts to ensure that clinical trials are designed to meet specific market needs and that this is conveyed to physicians prior to launch. To this end, developing and nurturing relationships with physician opinion leaders throughout the R&D process is critical. Firstly, this helps to determine unmet market needs, clinical trial design and product positioning. Secondly, and most crucially in the context of market penetration, such relationships drive product uptake upon launch, as opinion leaders will already be familiar with the product and its benefits (see Reuters 2003a).

Pre-launch marketing activities often include establishing advisory boards and sponsoring pre-launch conferences at which clinical trial results are presented to the wider medical community. However, they also include the direct involvement of leading physicians and medical establishments in clinical trials. By convincing opinion leaders of a drug's benefits, acceptance among late adopters can be accelerated. Early product branding further raises awareness among physicians prior to launch, increasing the likelihood of higher levels of initial uptake.

Raising pre-launch awareness also ensures that the needs of all stakeholders in the prescribing process are addressed before a product is launched. The payers' needs should also be attended to since they have the final say on price and reimbursement levels.

Even though pharmaceutical companies do not necessarily need to raise awareness of a product with payers in the same way as with physicians and patients, pre-launch preparation should include cost-effectiveness studies to demonstrate product value to payers. This is particularly important in publicly funded healthcare systems operating under extensive cost containment policies.

Conclusions

New markets are either not willing to pay the high prices common in the US and most European countries, or these markets are highly uncertain, difficult and expensive to develop. One new market in the US and European economies is geriatrics. People become increasingly older, and healthcare spending increases with age. For instance, average US Medicaid prescription drug spending was US$ 358 per enrollee, while the group of elderly accounted for about US$ 893 per enrollee. Thus, there are many new medicines under development that specifically aim at treating older people, targeting diseases such as diabetes, rheumatoid arthritis, Alzheimer's, depression, gastrointestinal disorders, osteoporosis, bladder/kidney disorders, or Parkinson's.

Despite potentially attractive profit margins and a favorable balance of power with respect to suppliers and product substitutes, the pharmaceutical industry is a tough one to be in. What used to be a safe haven for market leaders increasingly becomes a substitution market. While many diseases still await effective treatment, most of the obvious or easy drug targets have been discovered, and economically viable therapies have been developed. Start-ups and entrants employing new technologies compete with incumbent pharmaceuticals over international markets and new innovations.

Focusing on blockbusters appears to be an enviable competitive position, given the strong first-mover advantages in the pharmaceutical market. However, if a significant share of total sales depends on blockbusters, a company exposes itself to the risk of sharp sales drops once the underlying drug loses patent protection. Most pharmaceutical companies have thus started to balance and hedge their drug portfolios.

II. Pharmaceutical Innovation: The Case of Switzerland

Largest Economic Value-Added of GDP in Switzerland

Although we are going to focus on the Swiss pharmaceutical industry mostly, we will be referring to examples from both the pharmaceutical and the chemical disciplines for illustration, and will introduce the pharmaceutical industry in this wider context. The pharmaceutical industry originally emerged from the chemical industry. Still today, chemistry represents a significant part in the innovation of pharmaceutical products. There are a number of similarities in the production processes of both chemical and pharmaceutical substances. Many industry reports aggregate the chemical and the pharmaceutical industries into one single industry called 'the pharmaceutical-chemical industry'.

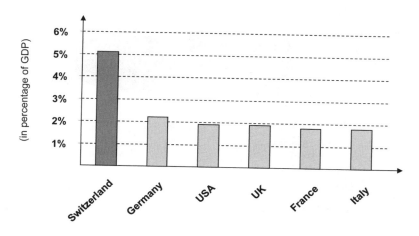

Source: BAK (2001)

Fig. 12. Economic value-added of the pharmaceutical-chemical industry in 2000.

In Switzerland, the pharmaceutical-chemical industry has turned out to be the major driver of economic wealth over the past years. A recent study revealed that the pharmaceutical-chemical industry significantly adds to economic wealth in Switzerland by contributing about 5% to the country's gross domestic product (BAK 2001). The pharmaceutical-chemical industry in most of the other European countries, as well as the US, accounts for only around 2% of GDP (see Fig. 12).

The Swiss pharmaceutical market was worth about CHF 3.4 billion in 2001*. Just the two largest Swiss pharmaceutical companies – Novartis and Roche – had aggregated total pharmaceutical sales of more than CHF 38.9 billion during the same period of time. The Swiss pharmaceutical industry is thus strongly export-oriented and highly global.

The pharmaceutical-chemical industry covers a broad range of different product categories, including vitamins, fine chemicals, plant protection agents, animal medicine, and specialty chemicals besides pharmaceutical products. However, pharmaceuticals account for the bulk of revenues in this industry. Fig. 13 shows the worldwide sales of the top 10 Swiss companies in the pharmaceutical-chemical industry broken down by product categories.

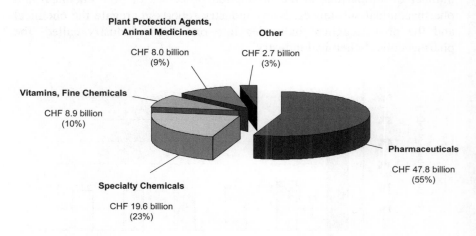

Source: SSCI (2000)

Fig. 13. Worldwide sales of the top 10 Swiss pharmaceutical-chemical companies in 1999.

---

* For currency conversion, the value of the US$ has dropped from about CHF 1.80 in 2000 to about CHF 1.40 in 2003.

Stable Market Growth

Switzerland as a growing lead-market

The Swiss pharmaceutical market has experienced significant growth over the past years by growing from CHF 2.3 billion in 1995 to CHF 3.4 billion in 2001 (Fig. 14). The world-market for pharmaceutical products has reached about US$ 352 billion in 2001 (IHA-IMS Health 2002), which was equivalent to about CHF 480 billion. Thus, the Swiss market represents 0.7% of the world-market. By 2002, worldwide pharmaceutical sales topped US$ 400 billion (PhRMA 2003), leaving the Swiss share of the world-market at about the same level.

While the increase in number of packs sold is basically stagnating between 180-185 million since 1995, the entire market in Switzerland grew at an average rate of 6.3% p.a. over the same period of time. Despite relatively high drug prices compared to neighboring countries, the Swiss pharmaceutical market is expected to grow at an average annual rate of 7.7% for the following five years (see Table 5).

According to data by IHA-IMS Health, there are 790 pharmaceutical companies active in the Swiss market. The three largest Swiss companies Novartis, Roche and Serono have an aggregated market share of about

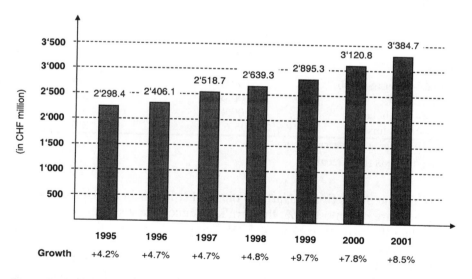

Source: IHA-IMS Health (2002)

Fig. 14. Development of the drug market in Switzerland (at manufacturers' prices).

Table 5. Swiss drug market growth rate forecast.

Year	Market Growth [in %]
2002	7.5
2003	8.0
2004	8.3
2005	7.5
2006	7.1

Source: IHA-IMS Health (2002)

18% of the domestic market. The eight largest foreign companies serve around 40% of the market in Switzerland, whereas large, foreign firms in total cover about 70% of the Swiss market. The remaining share of the market is served by small and medium-sized firms, which primarily cover the domestic generics market. The largest pharmaceutical companies in the Swiss market, including their sales and market share in Switzerland, are listed in the following table.

Table 6. Largest pharmaceutical companies in Switzerland in 2001.

Company	Revenues in Switzerland [*]	Market Share [in %]
Novartis	298.1	9.4
GlaxoSmithKline	261.1	8.3
Roche	233.1	7.4
AstraZeneca	224.1	7.1
Merck	206.0	6.5
Pfizer	167.5	5.3
Bristol-Myers Squibb	109.0	3.4
Pharmacia	100.6	3.2
Sanofi-Synthélabo	100.4	3.2
Johnson&Johnson	95.6	3.0

* in CHF million at manufacturers' prices

Source: IHA-IMS Health (2002)

While the Swiss firm Novartis is the market leader in Switzerland with a market share of almost 10%, the firm's revenues grew slower over the last year than the overall market, at 5.1% compared to more than 8% for the total market.

Worldwide, Novartis and Roche are ranked 7th and 13th in the pharmaceutical market (see also Table 4). The third-largest Swiss company Serono posted revenues of about US$ 1.25 billion in 2001 (about CHF 1.7 billion), putting it into 54th position worldwide (see Pharma Information

2002). Despite domestic market shares below 10%, Novartis and Roche are still the first and third largest competitors in Switzerland. Nevertheless, the most successful drugs are all exclusively produced by foreign firms, as shown in the following table.

Table 7. Most successful drugs in Switzerland in 2001.

Product (Company)	Revenues [*]	Market Share [in %]
Antra Mups (AstraZeneca)	76.0	2.4
Zocor (MSD-Chilbret)	44.8	1.4
Sortis (Pfizer)	43.8	1.4
Seropram (Lundbeck)	42.3	1.3
Norvasc (Pfizer)	34.3	1.1
Vioxx (MSD-Chilbret)	33.6	1.1
Augmentin (GSK)	26.8	0.9
Selipran (BMS)	26.4	0.8
Zyprexa (Eli Lilly)	23.9	0.8
Reniten (MSD-Chilbret)	23.5	0.7

* in CHF million at manufacturers' prices

Source: IHA-IMS Health (2002)

New product launches in the Swiss drug market have become more promising. While Swiss doctors were known for their reluctance to prescribe new products, this image has changed dramatically (Schlatter 2002). In 2001, 40% of total drug sales were products introduced on the market within the last 5 years.

The three major Swiss pharmaceutical companies Novartis, Roche and Serono are also major global players and sell their products worldwide. Due to the relatively limited size of the Swiss pharmaceutical market, Novartis, Roche and Serono are very active exporters of drugs.

Increasing export surplus

About 28% of drugs sold in 2001 in Switzerland (which represents sales of CHF 962 million at manufacturers' prices), have been produced in Switzerland. Of these, Novartis, Roche and Serono (also called the Interpharma companies) accounted for 60%, which is equivalent to 16.9% of the total Swiss pharmaceutical market (see Fig. 15).

About 72% of the drugs sold in Switzerland are imported. The Swiss Association of Importers of Proprietary Medicines (Vereinigung der Importeure Pharmazeutischer Spezialitäten, VIPS) reports that 70 companies are active in the Swiss pharmaceutical market. As already mentioned, they

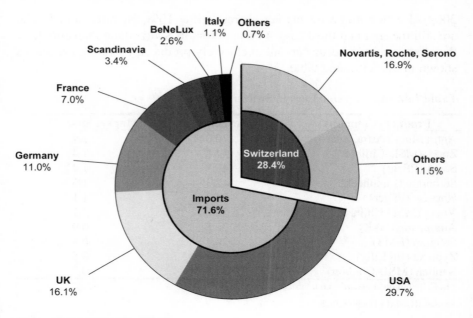

Source: Pharma Information (2002)

Fig. 15. Market share in Switzerland by country of origin in 2001.

are either subsidiaries of foreign pharmaceutical companies or Swiss pharmaceutical importers. In total, VIPS members and other importers posted revenues of around CHF 2.4 billion (at manufacturers' prices) in 2001.

The majority of imported pharmaceutical products sold on the Swiss market are from the USA (29.7%), UK (16.1%), Germany (11.0%), and France (7.0%). A much smaller number of imported pharmaceutical products is from Scandinavia, BeNeLux or Italy.

Due to the relatively small Swiss market compared to the large Swiss pharmaceutical companies, Switzerland has been posting a significant export surplus in pharmaceutical products for many years (Fig. 16). The value of exported Swiss pharmaceutical products has grown by a factor of three between 1990 and 2000. After balancing exports and imports, Switzerland earned an export surplus of CHF 14.0 billion on pharmaceutical products in 2001. More than 90% of the drugs manufactured in Switzerland are destined for export.

In 2001, pharmaceutical exports were valued at approximately CHF 27.7 billion. This corresponds to 66% of Switzerland's total chemical exports or 20% of the country's total export volume. The major recipients

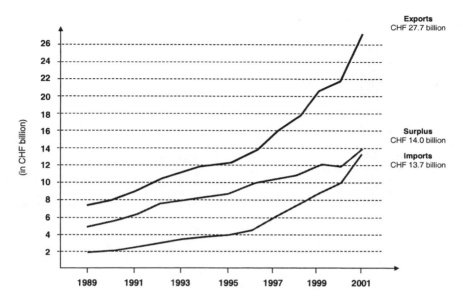

Source: Pharma Information (2002)

Fig. 16. Balance of trade for pharmaceutical products.

of Swiss pharmaceutical exports include Germany (14.8% of pharmaceutical exports), USA (10.9%), Italy (10.5%), France (9.6%), UK (5.5%), and Japan (5.3%). In absolute numbers, Europe is the largest buyer with CHF 18.1 billion, followed by the Americas and Asia.

The major sources of pharmaceutical imports into Switzerland include Germany (27.4% of pharmaceutical imports), UK (10.3%), Italy (9.3%), France (8.3%), USA (6.1%), and Japan (1.9%). In total, Europe represents 82% (or CHF 11.3 billion) of all pharmaceutical products imported.

When comparing the Swiss export surplus in pharmaceutical products with the rest of Europe (with a positive trade balance), we see that Switzerland leads not only in relative but also in absolute terms. While the comparison in Fig. 17 refers to data from 2000 – when Switzerland was posting a surplus of CHF 11.7 billion – the Swiss export surplus grew to CHF 14 billion in 2001 as mentioned earlier. Switzerland's positive trade balance is primarily due to the Swiss pharmaceutical industry's competitiveness in global markets. Despite its small size, Switzerland is the country that exports the highest volume of pharmaceutical products worldwide, ranked ahead of Germany. Both the USA and Japan had a negative trade balance for pharmaceutical products in 2000.

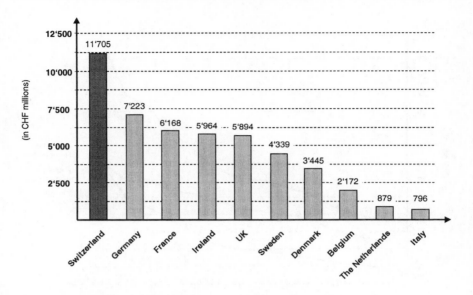

Source: Pharma Information (2002)

Fig. 17. International comparison of pharmaceutical export surplus in 2000.

Sound Productivity and Employment

Between 1995 and 2000 the productivity in the pharmaceutical-chemical industry in Switzerland grew at a real rate of more than 8% and reached a record high of CHF 210 per labor hour according to the Swiss Society of Chemical Industries (SSCI 2002). The productivity in the pharmaceutical-chemical industry is about four times higher than the average productivity across all Swiss industries. For example, the finance sector in Switzerland reached a productivity of CHF 100 per labor hour.

The pharmaceutical-chemical industry in Switzerland is highly productive also in international comparison. US productivity was around CHF 180 per labor hour while the most European countries reached a productivity of less than CHF 130 per labor hour. The high productivity in Switzerland allowed the pharmaceutical-chemical industry to pay relatively high wages and salaries (CHF 50 per labor hour). However, the primary reasons why wages and salaries with CHF 50 per labor hour are relatively low compared to the high productivity with CHF 210 per labor hour are due to the capital-intensive research and development expenditures in this industry.

The pharmaceutical-chemical industry is the second largest industrial employer in Switzerland with more than 68'000 employees in 2000. This represents about 10% of the total Swiss industrial workforce. 62% of employees in pharmaceutical-chemical companies are assigned to a higher category of qualifications by official statistics, compared to an average of 42% for all industries. 7'500 or 9% of all employees in the pharmaceutical-chemical industry are university graduates.

Within the pharmaceutical-chemical industry, the pharmaceutical industry has increased in importance at the cost of the chemical industry. The number of employees working for pharmaceutical companies rose from 22'200 to 25'800 between 1995 and 1998. In contrast, the workforce in the chemical industry declined.

Strong Support by Industry Associations

The pharmaceutical-chemical industry in Switzerland is organized in associations. Some of the major associations include SSCI, Interpharma, VIPS, and Intergenerika.

1. **SSCI:** The SSCI – the Swiss Society of Chemical Industries – is the main association in the Swiss pharmaceutical-chemical industry (Schweizer Gesellschaft für die Chemische Industrie, SGCI). Founded in 1882 and headquartered in Zurich, it is structured as an umbrella association. Around 220 industrial and commercial members are organized under the SSCI in 19 different areas. Each area focuses on one particular issue or product category. The SSCI itself belongs to national and international organizations, such as the Federal Commission for Drugs (Eidgenössische Arzneimittelkommission), the Section for Chemicals and Pharmaceuticals of the Industrial Department of the Federal Department for the Economic Accommodation of the State (Sektion für Chemie und Pharmazeutika des Industrieamts im Bundesamt für wirtschaftliche Landesversorgung), the European Council of Chemical Manufacturers' Federation (CEFIC) and the European Federation of Pharmaceutical Manufacturers' Associations (EFPIA), and many more.

   The SSCI represents the interests of its member corporations towards the government and the public by improving the long-term regulatory environment of its members both in Switzerland and abroad. The SSCI pursues the following objectives in the field of foreign trade:

- Creating underlying conditions for the world economy that are as liberal and stable as possible (e.g., within the framework of the WTO and the European Union);
- The removal of technical trade barriers through international harmonization of trade-relevant legal provisions in different countries, or via the mutual recognition of these provisions;
- Securing an appropriate recognition of corporate research efforts, including internationally improved protection of intellectual property.

2. **Interpharma:** Located in Basel, Interpharma is the association of the three largest Swiss companies involved in pharmaceutical research: Novartis, Roche and Serono. Created in 1933, Interpharma's board is comprised of one board member from each of the three firms as well as one additional person.

    Interpharma is engaged in establishing general conditions and frameworks within Switzerland and abroad, which strives to nurture innovation as well as support drug research and development. By establishing this association, the Swiss pharmaceutical firms expect to stay ahead and gain an edge over the worldwide competition. In addition, Interpharma tries to establish a positive social and political environment for pharmaceutical research.

3. **VIPS:** Another important association is the Swiss Association of Importers of Proprietary Medicines (Vereinigung der Importeure Pharmazeutischer Spezialitäten, VIPS). VIPS was founded in 1950 and includes today 70 member companies. VIPS-members are mostly Swiss subsidiaries of foreign pharmaceutical companies. As about 72% of all pharmaceutical products sold in Switzerland in 2001 were imports, VIPS represents a fairly important association for the entire industry. Hence, VIPS is engaged in both promoting the interests of importers towards government agencies as well as maintaining good relations and cooperations with other associations in the industry.

4. **Intergenerika:** Intergenerika represents the association of producers of generic drugs in Switzerland. Generic drugs are typically imitations of established drugs that are no longer protected by patents. As the market for generic drugs in Switzerland is growing rapidly, Intergenerika will probably become more important in the near future.

These four associations are the main lobbyists for the Swiss pharmaceutical industry. However, due to the impact of the bilateral contracts between Switzerland and the European Union as well as increasing efforts of the WTO, the national associations will have to adopt an increasingly European and/or international orientation.

Highly Global Orientation

Historically, the Swiss pharmaceutical-chemical industry has a strong international orientation. Swiss companies have been present in international markets for decades. Internationalization was necessary not only for large multi-product corporations but was also instrumental for many small and medium-sized enterprises that pursued niche strategies. Europe and America make up about 40% of the source of turnover, while Asia takes up about 17%, leaving Switzerland as a very small domestic market. Hence, worldwide marketing has always been an integral part of the Swiss companies' strategy.

The Swiss pharmaceutical-chemical industry has consolidated the international presence of its products since the beginning of this century by direct investments in more than 100 countries. The value of direct invest-

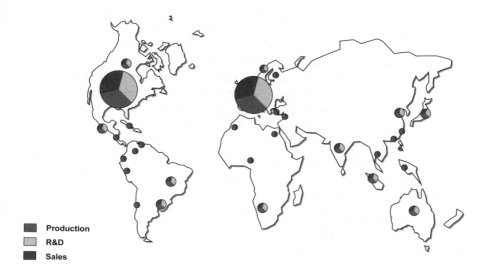

Source: Adapted from SSCI (2002)

Fig. 18. World map of R&D, production and sales of Swiss companies in 1998.

ments reached more than CHF 34 billion in 1998; a share of 40.7% of all direct investments made by the Swiss industry (Fig. 18).

Within Switzerland itself there is a geographic concentration of pharmaceutical-chemical companies on the northwest of Switzerland around Basel. About one quarter of total economic value in this region is created by the pharmaceutical-chemical industry. However, other Swiss regions are also important, most notably the Mittelland region (stretching from Zurich to Bern), the Lake Geneva area, and the Zurich metropolitan area becoming more and more attractive places for the pharmaceutical industry. Besides the northwest of Switzerland, these three regions have also evolved as centers of biotechnology activities due to their proximity to very good research centers within universities and companies.

Complex Industry and Product Classification

Industry definition

Despite the similarities between chemicals and pharmaceuticals, there is a general trend towards their separation into independent activities. Although there are still many companies that operate a pharmaceutical division side to side with a chemical division, capital markets increasingly require firms to separate these businesses. The reasons are found in higher profitability and lower exposure to cyclic trends in the pharmaceutical industry, which leads to a stronger shareholder value orientation.

The pharmaceutical industry is further broken down into several different therapy areas, which are also the base for organizational structure in most companies, like Roche and Novartis in Switzerland. The most common therapy areas in the Swiss pharmaceutical industry are shown in Fig. 19. Each therapy area covers several different product types.

The leading Swiss pharmaceutical companies Novartis, Roche and Serono occupy internationally important positions in the pharmaceutical industry with some of their most successful products, aiming at the following treatment opportunities:

- Anti-malaria drugs (Novartis and Roche);
- Antiviral drugs (Roche);
- Cancer drugs (Novartis and Roche);
- Cardiovascular diseases (Novartis and Roche);
- Cephalosporin antibiotics / anti-infectants (Roche);
- Dermatology, retinoides (Novartis and Roche);
- Diseases of the bones (Novartis);

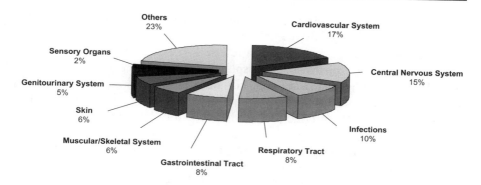

Source: Pharma Information (2002)

Fig. 19. Drug sales per therapy area in Switzerland in 2001.

- Diseases of the respiratory system (Novartis);
- Disorders of the central nervous system (Novartis);
- Drugs against AIDS (Roche and Serono);
- Endocrine disorders (Novartis);
- Growth disorder (Serono);
- Hematology (Novartis);
- Hormone replacement therapy (Novartis);
- Multiple sclerosis (Serono);
- Ophthalmology (Novartis);
- Parkinson preparations (Roche);
- Reproductive health (Serono);
- Rheumatism (Novartis);
- Transplants (Novartis).

Roche is also the world's leading manufacturer of diagnostic aids (clinical chemistry, immune chemistry, molecular diagnostic aids and patient care).

Product classification

By definition, pharmaceutical products (i.e., drugs) are 'substances or mixtures of substances, which are meant for use in the recognition, prevention or treatment of diseases or for some other medical purposes regarding influences on the human organism' (Leutenegger 1994). In general, drugs are differentiated into prescription drugs and non-prescription drugs. Further drug classifications include generic drugs, diagnostic drugs, orphan drugs or genetically manufactured drugs.

Prescription drugs are also often referred to as ethical drugs. They are only distributed by pharmacies, hospitals, or self-dispensing physicians. Self-dispensing physicians are very common in the Swiss pharmaceutical market. They do not just prescribe the respective drug, they are also allowed to dispense the product, which has typically been done by pharmacies or drug stores. However, the Association of Physicians with their own Dispensary (Vereinigung der Ärzte mit Patientenapotheke) now prefers to use the term 'Direct Dispensing of Medicines' (Direkte Medikamentenabgabe, DMA) instead of 'Self-dispensing' (SD) (see Pharma Information 2002).

Prescription drug sales at manufacturers' prices in Switzerland in 2001 increased by 10.3% from 2000 and accounted for about CHF 2.6 billion, which represents around 77% of total drug sales. The drugs were sold to pharmacies, self-dispensing physicians and hospitals.

Table 8. Prescription drug sales in Switzerland in 2001.

Distribution Channel	Revenues [*]		Number of Packs	
Pharmacies	1'413	(+7.3%)	41.3 million	(+0.5%)
SD-Physicians	664	(+18.4%)	20.2 million	(+8.6%)
Hospitals	534	(+9.0%)	17.4 million	(+1.2%)
Total	**2'611**	**(+10.3%)**	**78.9 million**	**(+2.6%)**

* in CHF million at manufacturers' prices

Source: Pharma Information (2002)

Non-prescription drugs can usually be purchased over the counter (OTC) at pharmacies and drugstores, or can be prescribed by SD-physicians or obtained in hospitals. Hence, non-prescription drugs include both medicines bought in pharmacies and drugstores without a prescription and medicines prescribed in medical practices and hospitals (see Pharma Information 2001). OTC drugs are also sometimes referred to as drugs purely used for self-medication purposes (i.e., without any prescription at all). OTC drugs are usually used for minor ailments such as headache or the flu.

Non-prescription drug sales accounted for CHF 773 million in Switzerland in 2001 or 23% of total drug sales respectively. This is equivalent to an increase of 2.8% compared to 2000 data. Pure self-medication drugs, drugs that can be purchased without any prescription at pharmacies or in drugstores, accounted for CHF 481 million or 14% of total drug sales in Switzerland.

Table 9. Non-prescription drug sales in Switzerland in 2001.

Distribution Channel	Revenues[*]		Number of Packs	
Pharmacies (w/o prescription)	336	(+3.7%)	46.2 million	(+1.3%)
Pharmacies (w/ prescription)	188	(+3.3%)	25.9 million	(+1.2%)
Drugstores	145	(-2.0%)	21.3 million	(-4.5%)
SD-Physicians	72	(+7.5%)	8.8 million	(+6.0%)
Hospitals	32	(+3.2%)	4.4 million	(+0.0%)
Total	**773**	**(+2.8%)**	**106.6 million**	**(+0.5%)**

* in CHF million at manufacturers' prices

Source: Pharma Information (2002)

Generic drugs are replications of prescription or non-prescription drugs where the patent protection has expired. Therefore, generic drugs (also referred to as generics) are usually offered by firms that did not develop the drugs themselves but gained a license to sell the drug. As these firms do not have to recoup high R&D expenditures, generic drugs are usually marketed at a lower price than the previous drug but have the same efficacy. Drugs that are about to lose their patent protection are thus exposed to severe competition. For instance, Eli Lilly's historic growth driver Prozac lost US patent protection in August 2001, and consequently, its sales declined by 66% in the fourth quarter of 2001 as a result of generic competition. Responding to the generic challenge, many pharmaceutical companies have started their own generics business. For example, Novartis is the largest generics company in the world.

The generics market in Switzerland has experienced significant growth. Generics have doubled their share of the pharmaceutical market since 1995 and reached sales of CHF 100.9 million at manufacturers' prices in 2001. However, the market share of generics compared to the total drug market in Switzerland has been relatively small at 3% in 2001 (Fig. 20). A reason could be that drug prices typically decrease significantly after a patent expires, which makes it economically very unattractive to sell generics. Another reason might be that manufacturers of generics just concentrate on drugs with a very high sales volume in order to reach a critical mass in sales and margins quickly.

With a current overall market share of 3% and 59.8% of all drugs being protected by patents, the remaining market-potential for generic drugs is about 37.2% of the total market. About three quarters of the potential market, which is equivalent to 27.5% of the total drug market, are characterized by original drugs whose patent protection has expired and no generics have been registered yet. Sales of drugs with expired patents, where generics already exist, accounted for about 9.7% of the total market.

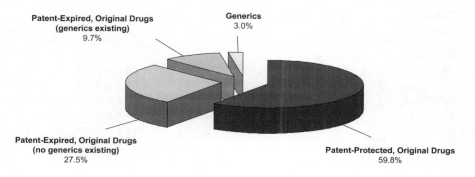

Source: Pharma Information (2002)

Fig. 20. Market share regarding patent protection in Switzerland in 2001.

Orphan drugs target rare medical conditions and thus provide the physician with therapeutic alternatives. In some cases, they even provide a first therapeutic option. The FDA grants orphan drug status to a company for a drug that is believed to substantially increase the life expectancy of the treated patient for a particular disease. This excludes other companies from receiving an FDA license to produce a similar drug for a finite period (usually 7 years), thereby allowing the company producing the drug to recuperate their R&D expenses.

For the pharmaceutical and biotech companies involved, the advantages are less apparent. Although legislation in markets such as the US, Japan, Canada, Australia and now Europe provides financial and development support to manufacturers. However, a company developing an orphan drug cannot expect to generate enormous profits, and the risks involved are still substantial. Hence, orphan drug legislation has consistently been perceived as being of principle advantage to the consumer. Besides providing exclusivity in a particular indication area or benefiting from other leveraging effects, orphan drugs can be used to improve the public profile of a company.

Genetically manufactured drugs play an increasingly important role in the pharmaceutical pipeline. Gene technology includes all methods to characterize and utilize genetic material and is used for drug discovery, research simulation, and even diagnostic purposes. The limitations of gene technology are mostly ethical.

Today, there are several genetically manufactured drugs available on the Swiss drug market. Sales of the 63 genetically manufactured products (55 drugs and 8 vaccines), which had been approved in Switzerland up to February 2002, accounted for CHF 159 million at manufacturers' prices in

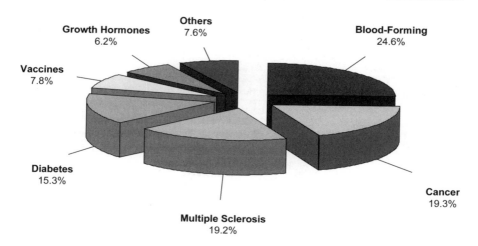

Source: Pharma Information (2002)

Fig. 21. Distribution of genetically manufactured products, by indication.

2001, up from less than CHF 20 million just a decade ago. Out of all genetically manufactured drugs, the majority of products are aimed at the therapeutic areas of blood formation (e.g., for treating myocardial infarction), with 24.6% of the market in terms of value, followed by cancer drugs with 19.3% and multiple sclerosis drugs with 19.2%. Vaccines accounted for 7.8% of total sales in this sector (see Fig. 21).

Fragmented Market Structure

All entities that interact on the Swiss pharmaceutical market can be classified as follows:

- Producers;
- Intermediaries and dealers;
- Consumers and financing entities.

Fig. 22 illustrates the entities and their respective relations including the flows of products, information and money. Therefore, pharmaceutical companies in Switzerland are targeting hospitals, medical doctors, wholesalers and self-dispensing physicians as potential customers. One result of the New Economy trend includes the opportunity of direct sales via the Internet. The Netherlands has emerged as a preferred supplier location.

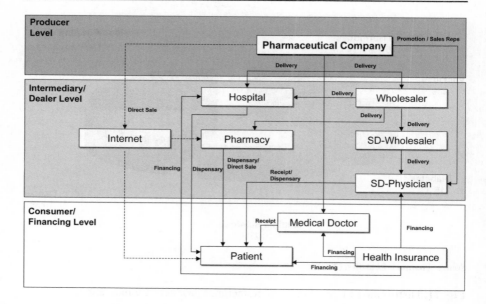

Source: Adapted from Leutenegger (1994)

Fig. 22. Market structure of the Swiss pharmaceutical industry.

Production

The market for producers of drugs is very fragmented. As already mentioned, 790 pharmaceutical companies are fighting for market share in Switzerland.

Only 28% of drugs sold in Switzerland are produced in Switzerland. Consequently, many subsidiaries of foreign pharmaceutical companies are active in the Swiss pharmaceutical market. However, these subsidiaries oftentimes have different functions. Some are just distribution companies with special registration competencies in Switzerland and some others are purely research labs. However, most foreign firms establish a presence in Switzerland in order to have direct access to the Swiss market and receive market permission from the Swiss regulation agencies (Leutenegger 1994).

In general, the manufacturers in Switzerland receive the lion's share of the drug's retail price. In 2000, the manufacturer of a pharmaceutical product received an average of 59% of the retail price, whereas 41% went to the wholesalers and retailers. However, a new 'performance-oriented' pricing structure will likely cause great changes in the pricing structure as described later on.

Distribution

Besides the Internet becoming a booming distribution channel for direct sales opportunities, the distribution network of the pharmaceutical industry in Switzerland has traditionally had two tiers. The first tier is comprised of wholesalers, who distribute the drugs to the second tier dealers. The second tier dealers have a more detailed distribution network. Typical second tier dealers are pharmacies, drugstores or SD-physicians. Hospitals usually use both systems, ordering directly from the pharmaceutical company or ordering from the wholesaler (Leutenegger 1994). The wholesalers only distribute drugs to firms or persons allowed to carry the respective drugs. This can be pharmacies, SD-physicians, drugstores or hospitals. Today, the following four major wholesalers are the eminent players on the Swiss market: Amedis, Galexis, Unione Farmaceutica, Voigt.

The CHF 3.4 billion spent on pharmaceutical products in 2001 are equivalent to 185.6 million packs of medicines. The drugs have been distributed via the following distribution channels noted in Table 10.

Table 10. Distribution channels in the Swiss pharmaceutical industry in 2001.

Distribution Channel	Revenues[*]		Number of Packs	
Pharmacies	1'937	(+6.2%)	113.4 million	(+1.0%)
SD-Physicians	736	(+17.4%)	29.1 million	(+7.8%)
Hospitals	567	(+8.8%)	21.8 million	(+1.4%)
Drugstores	145	(-2.7%)	21.3 million	(-4.9%)
Total	**3'385**	**(+8.5%)**	**185.6 million**	**(+1.3%)**

* in CHF million at manufacturers' prices

Source: Pharma Information (2002)

Drug sales at pharmacies have been rising steadily since 1990, while sales at drugstores have shown a slight decrease. In terms of value, 57% of all drugs were sold in 1'669 pharmacies in Switzerland in 2001. Between 1990 and 2001, 123 new pharmacies opened, while 182 drugstores closed. During the same period, the absolute number of SD-physicians rose by 587. In 2001, the Canton of Zurich alone registered an increase of 31 SD-physicians over the previous year (Pharma Information 2002).

SD-physicians are allowed to dispense pharmaceutical products in all cantons in Switzerland except for Ticino and West-Switzerland. Hence, the density of pharmacies is much higher in these two regions with 5.6 and 3.9 pharmacies respectively per 10'000 inhabitants. In turn, in areas where SD-physicians are allowed to dispense drugs, the number of pharmacies is relatively low, for example, there are only 0.9 pharmacies per 10'000 habitants in Central-Switzerland.

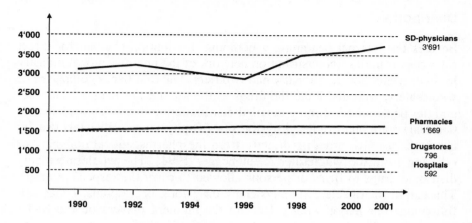

Source: Pharma Information (2002)

Fig. 23. Number of distribution outlets.

However, due to the liberalization of distribution channels and changes to the compensation model in the wholesale and specialist retail market (discussed later), the Swiss pharmaceutical market is undergoing massive changes. Under the influence of competition, the market structure with pharmacies, SD-physicians, hospitals and drugstores is developing differently.

For example, SD-physicians and pharmacies are increasingly in direct competition over customers. As SD-physicians are more and more taking market share away from pharmacies in their traditional fields, pharmacies have started to offer additional products and services, such as cosmetics, hygienics or even immunization services. Since July 2001, the performance-oriented compensation has also stimulated competitiveness among pharmacies and SD-physicians. According to the Handelszeitung (2002), every SD-physician earned on average about CHF 50'000-60'000 in 2001 from dispensing pharmaceutical products.

Consumption

The patient usually does not have much influence on a medical doctor's or physician's decision about a certain prescriptive drug, since their knowledge about the respective drug and its consequences tends to be limited. Moreover, the patient normally does not carry the costs for the product. These costs are typically covered by health insurance companies. As a consequence, the consumer (i.e., the patient) is less likely to develop a sense of cost consciousness regarding the pharmaceutical products being used. Hence, the product's quality is almost the only factor that influences the purchasing decision.

In accordance with a recent change in the national healthcare system, this is expected to change: The patient participates in the costs and, therefore, becomes more price sensitive. The informed patient is increasingly gaining in importance. The emergence of self-organized patient groups additionally requires pharmaceutical companies to shift more attention towards direct-to-customer or direct-to-patient marketing strategies.

In the case of non-prescription drugs (i.e., OTC drugs), the patients are usually able to select the drugs themselves. This leads to a higher cost-consciousness on the consumer's side. Health insurance companies are thus increasingly trying to market OTC drugs in order to reduce their reimbursement efforts.

In total, the average per-capita-spending on drugs in 2000 in Switzerland was CHF 433, based on manufacturers' prices.

Conjoined Financing Systems

While the Swiss market for healthcare services totaled more than CHF 43 billion in 2000, healthcare spending in Switzerland represented 10.7% of the country's Gross Domestic Product (GDP) in the same year. This proportion has risen 5.8 percentage points since 1970. In comparison to healthcare spending in other countries, Switzerland is in second place, behind the USA and before Germany (Fig. 24). Healthcare spending in the

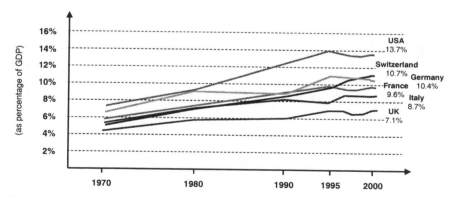

Source: OECD (2000)

Fig. 24. Healthcare spending as % of GDP.

USA is particularly high. In 2000, it amounted to 13.7% of the country's GDP. Since healthcare spending does not always cover the same elements in different countries, international comparisons are possible only to a limited extent.

When analyzing financial structures in healthcare, it is important to differentiate between parties who pay for the services and parties who finance the payments. The majority of healthcare costs have been paid by social insurance, totaling close to CHF 16.5 billion in 1999. Private households paid another CHF 13.8 billion and the remaining part was paid for by the public funds, private insurances and other funding. However, the actual burden of financing the payments fell on private households, whose contribution to healthcare funding rose to about CHF 27.8 billion in 1999. The remaining amounts were financed by public funds of CHF 6.8 billion, social security and social insurance of CHF 3.6 billion and CHF 3.3 billion respectively in 1999.

By further breaking down the CHF 43 billion in total healthcare spending in Switzerland, we see that drugs accounted just for about 10.7% or CHF 4.6 billion in 2000. In-patient treatment and out-patient treatment accounted for the largest part of healthcare spending with CHF 20.2 billion and CHF 12.8 billion respectively.

Only drugs included in the List of Proprietary Medicines (Spezialitäten-liste) published by the Federal Social Insurance Office (Bundesamt für Sozialversicherung) are covered by compulsory health insurance. The criteria for inclusion in this list relate not only to the drug's efficacy but also to its cost-effectiveness. This decision is made by the Federal Social Insurance Office, usually at the request of the Federal Drug Commission (Eidgenössische Arzneimittelkommission), which evaluates the cost-effectiveness of individual drugs based on their cost-benefit ratio.

In 2001, there were 7'046 drugs registered in Switzerland. Out of those, the List of Proprietary Medicine contained 2'499 drugs in 6'502 different packaging units. Close to eighty percent (79.9%) of the items were prescription drugs, while 20.1% were non-prescription drugs. In contrast, there were 4'547 drugs or 64.5% of all drugs not covered by the health insurance companies (see Fig. 25).

Strict New Drug Registration

The Swiss government is involved in the domestic pharmaceutical market in three different ways. First, in terms of actions regarding the drug's security and market accreditation. Second, in terms of price-regulation and,

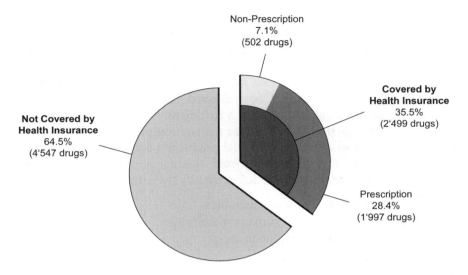

Non-Prescription
7.1%
(502 drugs)

Covered by
Health Insurance
35.5%
(2'499 drugs)

Not Covered by
Health Insurance
64.5%
(4'547 drugs)

Prescription
28.4%
(1'997 drugs)

Source: Pharma Information (2002)

Fig. 25. Health insurance covered products in 2001.

third, in terms of securing pharmaceutical know-how, such as patents. In general, if a pharmaceutical company is about to launch a new product into the market, several different policies and regulations have to be taken into consideration. The registration of the new drug is one of the first processes, and is supervised by Swissmedic.

Swissmedic, the Swiss Agency for Therapeutic Products, is a public institution within the Swiss government. It is affiliated to the Federal Department of Home Affairs. The legal basis for Swissmedic is the Swiss Federal Law on Medicinal Products and Medical Devices (Law on Therapeutic Products, LTP). The agency was formed in 2001 by a merger of the Intercantonal Office for the Control of Medicines (Interkantonale Kontrollstelle für Heilmittel, IKS) and the Therapeutic Products Section of the Swiss Federal Office of Public Health. Before the end of 2001, the Intercantonal Agreement (Interkantonale Vereinbarung, IKV) and the IKS, the IKV's executive organ, had been responsible for the investigation, appraisal and registration of all drugs sold on the Swiss market, as well as for the control of companies, which were producers or wholesalers of drugs. Since 2002, Swissmedic assumed these responsibilities.

Swissmedic's new area of responsibility takes into account the growing demands for international health protection and quality standards. At the outset, Swissmedic employs roughly 240 full-time employees.

Not only new drugs but all therapeutic products – including human and veterinary medicines and medical devices – are officially monitored by Swissmedic. This is expected to guarantee that only high-quality, safe and effective therapeutic products are placed on the market. When authorizing new medicines, Swissmedic bases itself on international licensing criteria. This means that drugs cannot be marketed in Switzerland unless their safety, efficacy and quality have been sufficiently demonstrated and verified. The overall goal of the new drug registration process is that the government agency can prove, by using the producer's documentation, that the drug's effectiveness, compatibility and quality is sufficiently demonstrated. Medicines required to be authorized by Swissmedic include:

- Synthetic prescription human medicines;
- Synthetic non-prescription human medicines;
- Complementary and herbal medicines;
- Biotechnological medicines;
- Veterinary medicines;
- Vaccines and blood products.

While the authorization procedure must be carried out and paid for by the company wanting to place the medicinal product on the market, Swissmedic's new drug authorization/registration process can be described by the scheme illustrated in Fig. 26.

The marketing company's application must contain all the scientific documentation necessary to assess quality, efficacy, and safety. Swissmedic checks the application to ensure its formal completeness. After this purely technical control measure, the second stage comprising the material assessment starts: with the help of an independent committee of experts, Swissmedic checks whether it is possible to prove the quality, efficacy and safety of the medicinal product on the basis of the documentation provided by the marketing company. A crucial part of this assessment is the positive risk-benefit ratio. This stage takes roughly six months, during which laboratory tests and clinical trials are evaluated on the basis of the documentation provided. During the third stage, Swissmedic analyzes the quality yet again, this time on the basis of samples of the medicinal product. Specialists carry out their own laboratory analyses. In addition, Swissmedic checks and amends the texts submitted as the information for professionals and patients (patient information leaflet).

Even before applying for the entire authorization procedure, Swissmedic checks whether the clinical trials have been carried out according to the recognized principles of good clinical practice. To protect trial subjects

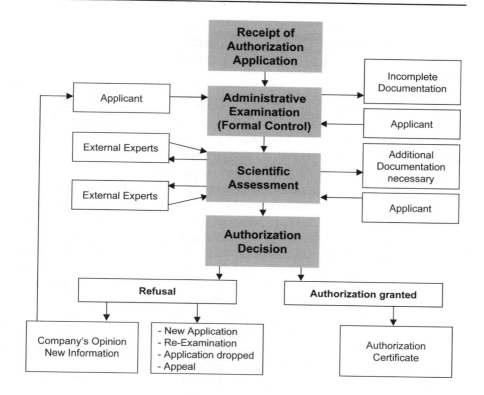

Fig. 26. New drug authorization/registration process at Swissmedic.

and patients, the agency must be notified of all clinical trials on therapeutic products.

Swissmedic works independently throughout the whole procedure; the manufacturer and potential marketer of the medicinal product, which is subject to authorization, has no influence over the procedure or its outcome. Swissmedic does not have access to the documentation or basis for decisions by European control agencies or the US Food and Drug Administration (FDA).

In comparison to the internationally well acknowledged procedures of the US Food and Drug Administration, the Swissmedic new drug authorization/registration process is slightly different. While Swissmedic only reviews the authorization application and assesses safety, efficacy and quality of drugs after the applying entity has handed in the application documents, the FDA's Center for Drug Evaluation and Research (CDER) interferes at two stages. The first is right after the pre-clinical tests, the CDER determines if the new drug is suitable for use in clinical trials. This process is called the Investigational New Drug (IND) Review Process. An IND permission has to be kept active annually by sending, for example, annual reports. In addition, projects are discussed with the FDA frequently, especially before entry into phase III clinical trials and submission. After the clinical tests have been successful, the CDER determines during a second step the benefit-risk profile of a new drug prior to approval for marketing. This process is referred to as the New Drug Application (NDA) Review Process. Hence, the FDA has a slightly stricter authorization procedure by intervening at two points during the drug development process.

In general, a high-quality test on pharmaceuticals is expensive and takes several months. However, the processing times for new drug authorizations in Switzerland are relatively short. Due to this efficiency, Switzerland usually belongs to the first group of countries in which a new pharmaceutical product will be authorized. As a general rule, the assessment of an application for authorization usually takes six months. After this time the marketing company is notified of the so-called preliminary decision, and eventually an authorization certificate is issued. The medicinal products can then be placed on the market. To ensure that particularly innovative medicines for life-threatening or debilitating diseases are made available quickly, a new accelerated authorization procedure was introduced in 1998. This so-called fast-track procedure enables Swissmedic to announce its preliminary decision after just three or four months.

The FDA also uses timesaving processes to speed up introduction of important new drugs to patients who need them. An accelerated approval may be granted to priority drugs that show promise in the treatment of serious and life-threatening diseases for which there is no adequate therapy. Treatment Investigational New Drug designations enable patients not enrolled in the clinical trials to use promising life-saving drugs while they are still in the testing stage. For example, when the first tests of the antiviral drug AZT in 1985 showed encouraging results in 330 AIDS patients, the FDA authorized a Treatment IND for more than 4'000 people with AIDS before AZT was approved for marketing.

The median length of time required to review and approve a new drug in countries other than Switzerland varies from 1.1 years in the UK to between 1.4 and 1.7 years in Germany, Australia, Spain, and the USA. A potential reason for the longer time needed in other countries could be, for example, that within the European Union, drugs must pass both national and EU regulatory reviews.

Only after a medicinal product has cleared all hurdles – and therefore fulfills the Swiss regulations regarding quality, efficacy, and safety – is it granted authorization. However, two points must be taken into consideration: first, this authorization must be renewed after five years; second, each medicinal product is classified according to lists. Depending on the relation between benefits and risk of the respective drug, Swissmedic is differentiating the drugs according to different lists, which also provide information about the dispension authorizations. The lists, along with their sales in percentage of total drug sales in 2001, can be characterized as follows:

Table 11. Lists of different types of drugs.

List	Description	Sales [*]
A	All drugs strictly by prescription	10.9%
B	All drugs by prescription	41.6%
C	All drugs not by prescription but only sold in pharmacies	11.5%
D	All drugs available in pharmacies and drugstores	33.3%
E	All drugs available everywhere	2.7%

* in percentage of total drug sales in 2001

Source: Pharma Information (2002)

Thus, about 53% of all drugs are only available by prescription (lists A, B). In general, this category system is expected to guarantee the necessary information and care for patients. In addition, after the authorization and registration process stage, this system serves as a point of reference for specialists and health insurance companies in knowing how to handle the medicine.

As already mentioned, there were about 7'000 drugs registered in Switzerland in 2001. All of the registered drugs can take on different forms, such as solid, semi-solid and liquid. Additionally, they can have different dosages, colors or tastes. In 2001, there were 9'147 different variants available on the market. Moreover, the packages can also have different sizes. Therefore, in total, there were 15'118 different pharmaceutical product-units available on the Swiss pharmaceutical market.

In general, it has to be considered that legal regulations most often reflect the entire society's position towards technology. In highly-developed industrial countries, a decline in public acceptance of new technologies, such as bio- and gene-technology, can be observed. Restrictive regulations for experiments on animals and stem cell research are typical examples. Thus, pharmaceutical companies might also consider regulations as a driver for shifting their research abroad.

Accurate Price Regulation

The Federal Social Insurance Office determines if a new product is to be included into the List of Proprietary Medicines. This list contains all pharmaceutical products that are recommended to the health insurance companies as reimbursable. The drugs on this list are subject to rigorous price-controls and economic feasibility studies. The Federal Social Insurance Office receives support from the Federal Drug Commission. This commission decides about the acceptance of a new drug into the List of Proprietary Medicines. The commission is comprised of a scientific and an economic council. As already mentioned earlier, the List of Proprietary Medicines covered 2'499 drugs in 6'502 package-units in 2001. Almost eighty percent (79.9%) were prescription drugs (sales category A and B) whereas 20.1% were non-prescription drugs (sales category C and D). 4'547 or 64.5% of all drugs were not covered by the health insurance companies (see also page 45).

Until mid-2001, the prices in the Swiss pharmaceutical market had been regulated by the so-called margin-order. The margin-order determined the distribution network and set the margins for each product on each distribution stage. The intention was to compete on the quality of the drugs and not on price. By focusing on quality instead of price, this system was expected to be more in the interest of the Swiss population's overall health. It is important to understand that the margin-order did not set the prices but only the respective margins. Prices had been set by the producers under surveillance of the predecessors of Swissmedic as well as the Federal Social Insurance Office.

After 1 July 2001, the industry association Sanphar along with the old margin-order have been replaced by the new performance-oriented compensation. The performance-oriented compensation covers all reimbursable drugs listed on the List of Proprietary Medicines. This ongoing shift towards a new compensation structure is expected to lead to significant changes. Instead of just compensating for the margin, which depends upon the original manufacturer's price, the new performance-oriented compensation is expected to compensate for the pharmaceutical performance of the pharmacy, drugstore, SD-physician or hospital. This means in particular that the compensation for drugs is decoupled from the price of the drug. Hence, neither the price nor the amount of the drugs should have an impact on the decision about the disposal of a certain drug. For example, a pharmacy which used to sell many expensive drugs, which in turn had to be reimbursed by health insurance companies, will not make as much profit as before and should have an incentive to sell more cost-appropriate prod-

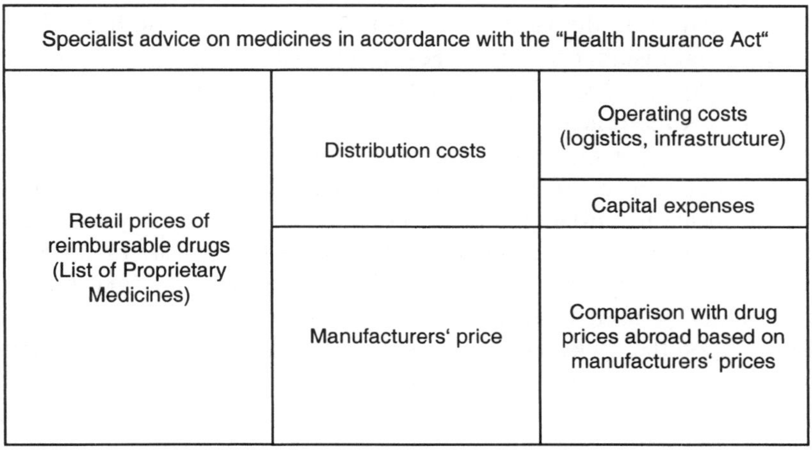

Specialist advice on medicines in accordance with the "Health Insurance Act"		
Retail prices of reimbursable drugs (List of Proprietary Medicines)	Distribution costs	Operating costs (logistics, infrastructure)
		Capital expenses
	Manufacturers' price	Comparison with drug prices abroad based on manufacturers' prices

Source: Pharma Information (2001)

Fig. 27. New compensation model for reimbursable drugs.

ucts, which is ultimately the goals of the so-called performance-oriented compensation. While this shift is expected to be cost-neutral over the short-term, it is expected to lead to significant cost-savings for the Swiss healthcare system over the medium- to long-term. In more detail, it is expected that low-end drugs will become slightly more expensive but, in turn, that high-end drugs will become significantly cheaper.

The changes include some of the following aspects. The basis for price comparisons with other countries was changed by the Federal Social Insurance Office, as was the method of defining the distribution costs. Price comparisons with other countries should now be made on the basis of manufacturers' prices (previously retail prices). Distribution costs now incorporate price-dependent capital expenses and operating costs (logistics, infrastructure). Retail prices for listed reimbursable prescription medicines (List of Proprietary Medicines) are now based on manufacturers' prices and distribution costs, and also include compensation for specialist pharmacy advice given by retailers, in accordance with the Health Insurance Act (Krankenversicherungsverordnung). The new price structure for reimbursable drugs is illustrated in Fig. 27.

Price increases for drugs on the List of Proprietary Medicines are regulated by the Federal Social Insurance Office as well. If a pharmaceutical company would like to receive a higher price for one drug, it has to file a respective application at the Federal Social Insurance Office. In general, price increases are only acceptable every two years. The only two factors that influence the evaluation of a potential price improvement are normal inflation as well as the sales development of the drug. Additionally, the Federal Social Insurance Office takes into consideration other drugs on the List of Proprietary Medicines, which belong to a similar therapeutic area and compares the prices with prices of a sample of other countries, which right now includes Germany, the Netherlands and Denmark. However, there is no general claim for a price increase. Price increases typically do not compensate for inflation and, hence, the drugs usually devaluate in real terms. Moreover, the price-supervisor for drugs on the List of Proprietary Medicines has a right for recommendation to the Federal Social Insurance Office, which he used several times in previous years.

Based upon the Swiss Health Insurance Act, the economic efficiency of all drugs on the List of Proprietary Medicines for more than 15 years has to be assessed. The economic efficiency of the respective drugs is also compared to foreign prices.

III.   The Science and Technology Challenge: How to Find New Drugs

Rise of the Biotechnology Industry: Boosting Innovation

Due to the enormous costs of building up a pharmaceutical R&D infrastructure, it was generally believed in the late 1970s and early 1980s that no new company would ever be able to enter the pharmaceutical industry and to compete with the industry's giants (see Robbins-Roth 2001). However, some entrepreneurs were not impressed with this challenge and created an entirely new industry – the biotechnology industry. Besides an innovative management approach as well as creative funding strategies, the main drivers for the rise of the biotechnology industry have been the emergence of new sciences and technologies. While innovation activities of established pharmaceutical companies were traditionally based on organic chemistry, biochemistry and chemical engineering, biotechnology companies have built a reputation in many novel areas, such as cell biology, molecular genetics, protein chemistry and encymology (Whittaker, Bower 1994).

The application of biotechnology in the pharmaceutical industry started with the development of scientific techniques, such as genetic engineering and antibody production. The technique of genetic engineering was developed in 1973, and received its first commercial pharmaceutical application four years later when Eli Lilly started the development of recombinant human insulin in cooperation with Genentech. The resulting product, Humulin, became the first biotechnology product when launched in 1983 (Reuters 2002).

By the end of 2000, a total of 76 biotechnology drugs had been approved for marketing, and 369 biotechnology drugs were in human clinical testing for more than 200 disease targets, accounting for around a third of all medicines in clinical development (Reuters 2002). A total of about 1'500 compounds were in the overall development stage around the year 2000 (Zanetti, Steiner 2001).

Following their launch, these early biotechnology products accounted for an average of 13.4% of all pharmaceutical products launched between

1991 and 1995, rising to 18.2% of all products launched between 1996 and 2000 (Reuters 2002).

However, just one out of 47 biotechnology companies possesses a successful product (Jakob 2003). Moreover, just 24 of the 3'000 biotechnology companies worldwide were profitable in 2000 (WGZ Bank 2002).

At the end of 2000, just four biotechnology drugs were considered blockbuster products and generated in excess of US$ 1 billion in sales: Procrit by Johnson&Johnson (US$ 2.7 billion), Epogen by Amgen (US$ 1.9 billion), Neupogen by Amgen (US$ 1.2 billion), and Humulin by Genentech and Eli Lilly (US$ 1.1 billion).

Due to the fact that most biotechnology firms have no product on the market yet and, hence, are heavily reliant on their research and development activities, they are of particular interest to established pharmaceutical companies' R&D. According to Reuters (2002), the advancement of biotechnology impacts the pharmaceutical value chain in two ways:

1. As the growth of new biotechnology product launches continues to outpace that of traditional pharmaceutical products, integrated pharmaceutical companies have established significant access to these new technologies through licensing agreements and alliances with biotechnology companies.
2. As the leading biotechnology companies have evolved through the development of key products, they have built up critical mass in the development and marketing functions in order to compete directly with the integrated pharmaceutical companies across the value chain.

According to Ernst&Young (2002), between 400 and 500 new alliances between pharmaceutical and biotechnology firms worldwide have been formed every year since 1996. The nature of these alliances varies: In some instances, a biotechnology shop exchanges an exclusive license to market and sell a patented drug to a pharmaceutical company that is willing to pay some research costs up front. Such agreements may also include limited use of the pharmaceutical company's manufacturing and distribution channels. In other instances, a pharmaceutical company makes a cash investment in exchange for a portion of future revenues and/or an equity stake in the biotechnology partner. This type of relationship is often tied to a marketing and distribution deal like the one described above. As a result, it is not unusual for a large pharmaceutical company to have biotechnology holdings that give them a substantial piece of the action: Novartis, for instance, owns about 40% of Chiron, and Roche owns about 60% of Genentech.

Recent research on alliances between biotechnology and pharmaceutical firms suggests that alliances are becoming more sophisticated and mature, that drug companies are poles of the alliance networks, and that new biotechnology firms play a mediating role in transforming scientific knowledge into patented technologies (see Lin 2001).

Biotechnology as a major input for pharmaceutical R&D has also become an important and rapidly growing sector in Switzerland. Between 1998 and 2000, the number of pure biotech-firms has more than doubled from 70 to 130. In 2003, Switzerland had the fifth largest biotechnology market in Europe. Including the biotechnology departments of pharmaceutical companies and firms that produce, for example, instruments aimed at the biotechnology industry, this sector generated revenues of CHF 3 billion and created an economic value of CHF 1.7 billion, which is equivalent to about 0.4% of the overall economic value creation in Switzerland. Biotechnology companies include large multinationals and small university start-ups, with firms conducting R&D in almost all areas of life sciences. In total, about 8'900 people are employed in the biotechnology industry in Switzerland.

The Swiss government has demonstrated a relatively strong commitment to the biotechnology industry with the establishment of the Swiss Priority Program Biotechnology in 1992 and a new funding program for the National Centers of Competence in Research. The Swiss Priority Program Biotechnology allocated over CHF 78 million in the areas of pharmaceuticals, process technology, food and plant biotechnology, bioelectronics, biosafety and neuroinformatics. The program has emphasized technology transfer and has led to the widespread exchange of knowledge and technology between universities and private industry. The funding program for the National Centers of Competence in Research provides about CHF 59 million specifically for research in the life sciences. Projects funded include research programs in molecular oncology, 3D structure and interaction of molecules, neural plasticity and repair, and computer/image guided medical interventions (see Standort Schweiz 2003).

More than 300 research groups in Switzerland's public institutions are active in the field of biotechnology, many of whom are involved in international research programs. In addition, there are numerous government and private resources available to support the creation of spin-off companies and assist in developing efficient patent and licensing strategies. While there were several successful venture capital fundings of Swiss biotechnology firms in 2001 – including one successful IPO – several Swiss biotechnology companies are waiting for the next IPO window to open up (see Ernst&Young 2002).

Swiss public biotechnology firms had 24 products in the product pipeline that were tested at the time of writing and were expected to enter the market in the near future. Compared to other European countries, Switzerland is ranked number 4 behind the UK with 154 products, Denmark with 33 products and France with 27 products in the product pipeline. German public biotechnology firms rank seventh with 11 products in the product pipeline (Ernst&Young 2002).

Cytos Biotechnology: Innovation made in Switzerland

Founded in 1995 as a spin-off of the Swiss Federal Institute of Technology (ETH) in Zurich, Cytos became a publicly listed biotechnology company in October 2002. Today, in 2003, Cytos employs 115 people, 45 of them holding a Ph.D. In addition, Cytos' CEO, Dr. Wolfgang Renner, won the Swiss Entrepreneur-of-the-Year Award in 2000.

The scientific foundation for Cytos' strategy is the product-platform concept. Cytos applies its integrated technology platform across a broad range of disease areas to maximize opportunities for product development and to build a versatile portfolio of novel therapeutic molecules.

Cytos' core competencies revolve around working with proteins. Cytos' Immunodrugs™ represent a new class of biopharmaceuticals that are designed to instruct the patient's immune system to produce a desired therapeutic antibody or cytotoxic T cell response to reverse or prevent disease progression. This approach represents a paradigm shift away from passive immunization towards an active immunization of the patient against a disease-related protein and combines the hallmarks of classical pharmacology with vaccination.

The current IP portfolio of Cytos comprises of four issued patents and 29 pending US patent applications (two of which are jointly owned with a partner) directed to Cytos' technology platforms and derived products, as well as the corresponding foreign patent applications. In addition, two patents and one patent application are in-licensed.

Due to increased competition from biotechnology companies, which are coerced into using the latest drug discovery techniques in order to survive in the market, every pharmaceutical company is facing the pressure to be amongst the technological leaders in their respective area. The following paradigm shift was observed in the past: Traditional approaches and sequential experimentation in drug discovery have increasingly been complemented by automated, mass-production analyses of compound libraries and computer-based experimentation using several different new technologies. In addition, the discovery of the Human Genome is expected to further supplement this paradigm shift in pharmaceutical R&D. While more than 500 biological targets for drugs have been identified so far, it is estimated that the Human Genome Project will produce another 3'000 to 10'000 new targets (Pfeiffer 2000).

The application of new sciences and technologies will lead to the following essential changes and impacts on the drug discovery process (see also Nightingale 2000):

- The nature of scientific understanding of diseases becomes more fundamental. A more detailed understanding of drug target function in the context of a molecular mode of disease onset, progression and chronicity will increase the quality of applied targets;
- The scale of experimentation undergoes fundamental changes and shifts from an individual initiative to an automated mass-production process;
- The cycles of trial and error experimentation are complemented by computer simulations;
- Complementary screening is performed by computer simulations;
- Single compounds are replaced by compound libraries;
- Structural complexity and diversity of compound libraries are expected to increase.

This chapter focuses on new sciences and technologies as the underlying drivers for innovation in the pharmaceutical industry (see Fig. 28). They enable the different parts of pharmaceutical research and development and lead to significant and revolutionizing results in pharmaceutical innovation.

The highest potential for improvement lies in the early research phases. For example, in 1998, Hoechst paid about DM 1 billion (about €500 million) for a single gene technology owned by a small company. In the later phases, R&D costs can escalate dramatically; up to 80% of total R&D expenditures can be incurred during the clinical stages. Therefore, new sciences and technologies are expected to have the largest impact in early-stage research.

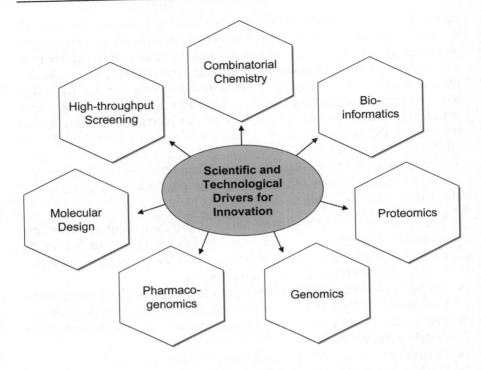

Fig. 28. New sciences and technologies as drivers for innovation.

High-Throughput Screening: Fail Earlier, Succeed Sooner

High-throughput screening (HTS) or ultra high-throughput screening (UHTS) belong to a wide range of novel drug discovery technologies, which are revolutionizing pharmaceutical research.

„These new plate formats have arisen as a potential answer to the problematic question being asked at most major pharmaceutical companies: How can we screen more targets and more samples cheaply?" (Houston, Banks 1997).

The consistent application of novel drug discovery technologies allows for the automation of much of the discovery function, promoting a more comprehensive and consistent screening process. Both the quality and quantity of resultant lead compounds are expected to increase. The overall goal of improving the early phase in drug discovery is to identify promising chemical samples or entities as soon as possible. The guideline here is to ‚fail earlier in order to succeed sooner'.

In the 1990s, high-throughput screening became the major tool for lead identification. HTS is the biological technology that allows large numbers of chemicals to be automatically tested for their impact on biological activity, representing components of disease. It comprises of a system for data handling, an array of compounds to be tested, a robot to perform the testing and a biological test configured for automation.

As a result, the yearly throughput of a typical lead discovery group increased from about 75'000 samples tested on about 20 targets to over a million samples tested on over 100 targets (Houston, Banks 1997). Today, UHTS allows for simultaneously screening of more than 100'000 substances per day in a fully automated way. Some companies achieved improvements in screening effectiveness well above a multiple of 25 by using HTS and UHTS technologies (see Reuters 2002).

While the quantity of screened substances is increasing tremendously, the screening technologies, however, do not have an impact on the quality of the outcome. Besides screening through a vast number of substances, it is therefore equally important to have the right substances included in the pool of all substances that are to be screened.

Combinatorial Chemistry: Cut Experimental Cycle Times

Along with high-throughput screening, combinatorial chemistry is considered to be one of the most essential tools for drug discovery. The two technology platforms of combinatorial chemistry and HTS account for more than half of all spending on new discovery technologies in the pharmaceutical industry (Reuters 2002).

The emergence of combinatorial chemistry was triggered by the increasing application of HTS technologies. With the surge of high-throughput screening technologies, a bottleneck in the discovery process occurred as the production of compounds did not expand at the same rate. With a shift from being able to screen hundreds of compounds to being able to screen tens-of-thousands of compounds in the early 1990s, it became obvious that pharmaceutical firms could test all their compounds very quickly. Hence, improvements in screening technologies increased demand for compounds and created a 'reverse salient' in synthetic chemistry (Nightingale 2000). A new technology had to fill this vacuum.

Combinatorial chemistry is a technology that allows large numbers of compounds to be made by the systemic and repetitive covalent connection of a set of different 'building blocks' of varying structures to each other. This helped pharmaceutical research be able to yield a large array of diverse molecular entities. Hence, combinatorial chemistry is a mass-production technology that synthesizes large numbers of compounds in parallel.

Combinatorial chemistry has reduced experimental cycle times by more than eight hundred times and lowered costs and risks by more than six hundred times compared to traditional methods (Booz Allen & Hamilton 1997).

While HTS and combinatorial chemistry are definitely major improvements in pharmaceutical research, these technologies remain relatively novel and their transition into launched products is yet to be seen. It is not surprising that many experts today still believe that serendipity is a key success factor.

Bioinformatics: More than 100 Gigabyte of Data per Day

"You have 50'000 to 100'000 genes in the body, and each cell expresses a subset of those genes. We take the RNA from those cells and make copies, called cDNA. Those copies are put into what we call expression plasmids and then put into bacteria, so we have hundreds of thousands of these bacteria all with one specific cDNA sequence to form what is called a 'library' of cDNA clones."

Dr. Raymond Goodwin,
2001 Winner of the PhRMA Discoverers Award

Bioinformatics generally deals with the acceleration of lead discovery by providing structural data, information and knowledge. The worldwide amount of knowledge doubles every seven years (Davis, Botkin 1994). The number of scientific journals was 100 at the beginning of the 19th century, 1'000 around 1850, over 10'000 in 1900; by 2000 there were around 100'000 worldwide. Today, over 5 million people work in the area of knowledge production in R&D departments – approximately 90% of all scientists who have ever lived (Nefiodow 1990; Pfiffner and Stadelmann 1995). Pharmaceutical research is among the leaders in knowledge production. Drivers for the increasing knowledge accumulation include the escalating usage of novel drug discovery technologies as well as external knowledge acquisition.

New technologies in drug discovery produce huge amounts of valuable data and information, which have to be processed and prepared in order to be accessed during the pharmaceutical innovation process. New methods and technologies are necessary to make use of this knowledge. Given that a single pharmaceutical lab can generate more than 100 GB of data per day, this job can only be done by sophisticated information technologies.

In addition, research is increasingly conducted externally. For example, Merck stated in its 2000 annual report that its own research accounts for only 1% of the biomedical research in the world. In order to tap into the remaining 99%, the company has to actively reach out to universities, research institutions and companies on a global scale to bring the best of technology and potential products into Merck. The cascade of knowledge flowing from new sciences and technologies is simply far too complex for any one company to handle alone. Toward that end, Merck has now challenged its internal scientists with a new task: to create a virtual lab in their research area. This means that Merck scientists do not just create excellent science in their own lab; instead, they identify and build connections to excellent science in other labs, wherever these labs may be (see Chesbrough 2003). Hence, efficient knowledge acquisition and effective integration in the scientific community becomes increasingly important. Even small start-up companies operate relatively globally in R&D: They acquire their knowledge through cooperation with other complementary companies as well as through public databases (e.g., Internet).

Consequently, information technologies in pharmaceutical research have to deal with both the management of data and knowledge within the corporate boundaries as well as the linkages to the outside research community. Baumann (2003) summarizes the major tasks of information technologies in pharmaceutical R&D as follows:

- To provide and manage databases for the tremendous amount of information;
- To allow the generation of compound profiles for improved target identification and screening;
- To manage genome and protein sequences;
- To visualize 3D data;
- To collect data on model organisms;
- To manage the huge amount of data from the clinical tests and provide feedback to the early phases of drug discovery;
- To enable accessibility and sharing of knowledge within the corporation as well as to outside collaborators.

One of the foremost tasks of information technologies in pharmaceutical research is to handle the large amounts of complex data generated throughout all phases of the R&D process. Recent improvements have been seen in data management software, statistical analysis software and the visualization technologies required to illustrate and represent the bulk of data. In the past, computer programs dealt only with single molecules and/or compounds. Today – by having compound libraries – it is possible to compare and explore patterns within the collections of compounds. Compound libraries can also be tested against counterscreens by using statistical techniques to understand why a molecule is selective for a particular substrate. Hence, data is stored and used to help re-analyze new data. This allows a more detailed understanding of the structure-activity relationship (see also Nightingale 2000). The comprehensive and complex databases also allow to determine the value of purchasing compounds. Clinical trial design can also be improved through a superior understanding of how a drug is likely to act.

The Internet will emerge as a key tool and will provide pharmaceutical companies with the ability to more effectively interact with partners, regulators and consumers. Internet-based technologies hold the potential to impact every stage of the pharmaceutical value chain. The ability to access and share data, and to interact and communicate within and across organizations, will determine how successfully new technologies are integrated. Investment in Internet technologies should realize significant productivity gains across the research and the development functions.

A recent survey among R&D executives conducted by Accenture showed that 54% of respondents agreed that new Internet technologies are fundamentally changing R&D processes (Accenture 2001b). 86% believed these technologies would have a great impact in the near future, while 58% said that there is already a high level of urgency within their organizations to adopt new technologies. However, barriers to the adoption of new Internet technologies included concerns over the security of company proprietary information, regulatory concerns about patient confidentiality, and budget and staffing issues.

In summary, bioinformatics is expected to lead to very valuable improvements in the early stages of pharmaceutical research. By using increasingly sophisticated information technologies in the early phase, economies of scale therefore become less important.

Proteomics: Profiting from the Human Genome Project

The term proteome refers to all the proteins expressed by a genome, and proteomics is dealing with proteins produced by cells and organisms. The approximately 30'000 genes defined by the Human Genome Project translate into 300'000 to 1 million proteins when alternate splicing and post-translational modifications are considered. While a genome remains unchanged to a large extent, the proteins in any particular cell change dramatically as genes are turned on and off in response to its environment.

Most drugs work on proteins or protein receptors. Hence, a primary challenge of proteomics is to identify differences between the pattern of a healthy and a sick person, compare them, and identify and isolate the guilty proteins. Consequently, proteomics covers efforts to obtain complete descriptions of the gene products in a cell or organism. Today, proteomics includes not only the identification and quantification of proteins, but also the determination of their localization, modifications, interactions, activities, and, ultimately, their function.

It is generally believed that through proteomics new disease markers and drug targets can be identified that will help design drugs for the prevention, diagnosis as well as treatment of diseases. While the future of biotechnology and medicine will be impacted greatly by proteomics, there is much yet to do to realize the potential benefits.

Several difficulties arise when studying proteins. Proteins are more difficult to work with than DNA and RNA. Proteins cannot be amplified like DNA, therefore less abundant sequences are more difficult to detect. Proteins have secondary and tertiary structures that must often be maintained during their analysis. Proteins can be denatured by the action of enzymes, heat, light or by the impact of physical forces. Some proteins are difficult to analyze due to their poor solubility.

As protein identification and characterization technologies are improving, the bottleneck in proteomics will be shifting from generating proteomic information to applying it.

Genomics: Towards Individualization and Mass Customization

> „As the genomic revolution continues, we will invent medicines we could not even envision just a few years ago. "
>
> Henry A. McKinnell, Jr.,
> President and CEO, Pfizer, 2002

Genomics describes the process of identifying genes involved in diseases through the comparison of the genomes of individuals with and without disease. Genomics is the most high profile of the many enabling technologies recently developed in pharmaceutical R&D. It has been heralded as having the potential to revolutionize both medicine and the entire pharmaceutical industry. Genomic technologies will enable the identification of 3'000 to 10'000 new drug targets, compared with the current number of 500 (Pfeiffer 2000). The integration of genomics and other technologies will lead to a shift from broadly targeted drugs to more focused medicines with much higher therapeutic value for the target population. Genomics is the pharmaceutical answer to mass customization: Realizing economies of scale with individualized drugs.

While genomic technologies allow for a better understanding of drug target function in genomic population subsets, or even individuals, it raises great commercial and financial concerns. The time and resources that must be spent to develop genetic profiles and market sizes for tailored drugs are much smaller, resulting in the need for completely different portfolio management strategies. Exploiting this opportunity will require that companies leverage genotype-based diagnostics into personalized medicine, completely shifting the end-game equation from high-volume/high-value (e.g., blockbuster drugs) to small-volume/higher-value (individualized) drugs. While some believe that personalized medicine will be of limited importance, others are convinced that it will have a broad impact in the industry and further, that using genotype-based elimination/exclusion of major side effects will actually create even larger blockbuster products than is possible based upon today's approach in developing and prescribing medicines (Accenture 2001a).

New genomic biology has accelerated the process of discovering novel targets, but a certain lack of maturity still characterizes technologies such as functional genomics, which play critical roles in determining the biological functions of targets, and in translating knowledge into drugs. Validation of the many targets generated by genomic methods is the major bottleneck in drug discovery together with the structural complexity and diversity of screenable compounds.

The use of genomics beyond target generation has generated great interest, but there is no clear picture yet as to how to best utilize genetics for value creation. According to research by Reuters (2002), the application of disease genetics and pharmacogenetics together could, in the very best case, save as much as two-thirds on the current cost to develop a drug.

The genomic revolution began in 1993 when Human Genome Sciences formed its partnership with SmithKline Beecham. However, it was not until the completion of the first draft of the human genome was announced in 2000 that the accompanying media and investor attention suggested that genomics had become an essential investment for achieving effective drug discovery in the future. No major pharmaceutical company is now without genomics capabilities, whether in-house or accessed through licensing agreements.

For certain organizations, external sourcing of genomics capabilities is a viable long-term strategy. Many drug companies are establishing numerous alliances with genomics focused players to complement their internal capabilities. In 1999, 381 genomics deals were reported (Accenture 2001a).

Most genomics companies do not usually provide full disclosure of their R&D pipelines. Hence, it is very difficult to assess the current impact of genomics on the pharmaceutical industry. In addition, some very high profile companies, including Incyte and Myriad, do not publish details of the success of their collaborations in terms of generating leads. Similarly, pharmaceutical companies with extensive in-house genomics expertise, such as Novartis and GSK, do not publish details of their early stage research.

Over 2'500 new targets have been discovered by genomics companies by 2001, assuming no duplication. With a minimum of 49 products in preclinical development and at least 13 already in clinical trials, the productivity of the genomics industry seems to be strong (Reuters 2002).

Lehman Bros. estimated that it requires a US$ 100 million annual investment to participate in the genomics arena. To compete in the more aggressive game of an emerging technology, a company might require up to US$ 300 million annually (Agarwal et al. 2001). With an average integrated pharmaceutical company spending around 25% of R&D on discovery, an aggressive investment in new technologies would consume more than 75% of a middle-tier company such as Roche or Schering-Plough's discovery budget, and would still consume 30% of a top-tier company's budget such as GlaxoSmithKline or Pfizer (Reuters 2002).

At the time of writing, the returns on investment of genomic activities are still uncertain. Tremendous uncertainty about the eventual 'best play' scenario in the genomics environment acts as a 'leveler' between the established integrated pharmaceutical companies and the emerging genomics-based companies. The intellectual capital advantage of the highly specialized genomics-based companies may provide them with distinct advantages over larger integrated companies.

The genomic revolution impacts the pharmaceutical value chain in three ways: First, the upside potential of genomics has led to an intensified wave of investment by the integrated pharmaceutical companies, resulting in increased licensing agreements and alliances with genomics-based companies. Second, the level of investment required to fully integrate genomics knowledge and technologies extends competitive advantages for the top-tier global pharmaceutical companies through their ability to access capital. Third, uncertainty over the eventual impact of genomics is creating something of a level playing field for future competition within the pharmaceutical industry. The eventual costs and benefits could help towards redistributing the balance of power between the integrated pharmaceutical and the specialized genomics-based companies (Reuters 2002).

Pharmacogenomics: Create Tailor-made Drugs

Pharmacogenomics describes how an individual's genetic inheritance affects the body's response to drugs. Pharmacogenomics combines traditional pharmaceutical sciences such as biochemistry with annotated knowledge of genes, proteins, and single nucleotide polymorphisms. The term is derived from the words pharmacology and genomics and is thus at the intersection of pharmaceuticals and genetics. Hence, pharmacogenomics is a discipline that primarily deals with the production of tailor-made drugs for individuals. The drugs are then expected to be adapted to each person's own genetic makeup. Environment, diet, age, lifestyle, and health all can influence a person's response to medicines, but understanding an individual's genetic makeup is thought to be the key to creating personalized drugs with greater efficacy and safety.

Currently, physicians prescribe medication through a trial-and-error method of matching patients with the right drugs. If the prescribed medication does not work for the patient the first time, the physician will try a different drug or dosage, repeating the process until the patient improves. As pharmacogenomics becomes more advanced, physicians eventually will be able to prescribe medication based on an individual patient's genotype, maximizing effectiveness while minimizing side effects.

In discovery, pharmacogenomics may facilitate targeting, understanding of disease pathways, and design of interventions for diseases with multiple genetic etiologies (e.g., breast cancer); along with variants of the same gene in a disease pathway. Differences in genes can also impact drug kinetics, (i.e., absorption, distribution, metabolism and elimination). In development, pharmacogenomics may improve the success rate of clinical trials through use of patient subsets with specific genetic risks and reduced chances of toxicities and side effects (Accenture 2001a).

Once pharmacogenomics provides tailored drug therapy based on genetically determined variation in effectiveness and side effects, the major benefits could be as follows:

- More powerful medicines;
- Better, safer drugs the first time;

- More accurate methods of determining appropriate drug dosages;
- Advanced screening for disease;
- Better vaccines;
- Improvements in the drug discovery and approval process.

Finally, pharmacogenomics is expected to lead to an overall decrease in the cost of healthcare due to decreases in:

- The number of adverse drug reactions;
- The number of failed drug trials;
- The time it takes to get a drug approved;
- The length of time patients are on medication;
- The number of medications patients must take to find an effective therapy;
- The effects of a disease on the body (through early detection).

Molecular Design: From Experimenting to Analytic Design

While the targets of most drugs are proteins, the molecular design of drugs – also referred to as rational design – tries to discover new drugs by looking at the structure of the underlying proteins. By contrast, most other new drug discovery technologies, such as high-throughput screening or combinatorial chemistry, rely upon screening through vast inventories of naturally occurring and man-made chemicals, in search of previously undiscovered substances with the desired biological activity. Lead-optimization is mostly achieved by random exploration of the chemical structure through the synthesis of large numbers of chemical derivatives. While this approach has already tremendously improved the pace of drug discovery, many important therapeutic needs remain for which screening-based research has failed to yield acceptably safe and effective drugs.

While all of the novel screening methods are trying to find the relevant substances by eliminating the irrelevant substances, molecular drug design is analytically deriving the design of the target molecules. The latter approach seems to be far more effective and efficient than screening methods because it is based on an analytical process rather than serendipity.

The basic rationale of how almost all drugs work is well known: Nearly every drug works through an interaction with the target molecule or protein, which causes the respective disease. The drug molecule inserts itself into a functionally important crevice of the target protein, like a key in a lock. The drug molecule is then connected to the target and either induces or, more commonly, inhibits the protein's normal function.

Consequently, a better and more direct understanding of the drug-target interaction would make screening through hundreds of thousands of substances obsolete. If it is possible to identify, in advance, the appropriate target for a given therapeutic need including the structure of the target protein, the structure of an ideal drug molecule could easily be designed to interact with the respective target.

Hence, molecular design is involved in exploiting three-dimensional structures of molecular targets as well as the respective drug molecules. X-ray crystallography in conjunction with genetic engineering techniques are typically used to identify, purify, and modify appropriate proteins. High-speed computers with sophisticated software tools are needed, which permit chemists to predict and simulate molecular structure, dynamics and energetics.

After determining the three-dimensional atomic architecture of the target protein and its functionally critical regions, a variety of specialized programs on interactive graphics workstations come into play. A design team develops and evaluates ideas for structures of drug molecules that complement the unique structure and electronic environment of the target protein. The medicinal chemists then chemically synthesize the most promising candidate structures. As in conventional drug discovery strategies, biochemists measure the ability of these newly synthesized drug candidates in order to produce the intended effect upon the target protein. Crystallographers then re-determine the structure of the protein target – now in combination with the candidate drug molecules. They see the detailed structural interactions actually achieved by the candidate drugs with their target. The scientists relate the performance of such compounds measured by familiar biochemical techniques to its structural interactions with the target as revealed crystallographically. The design team then incorporates the results of this analysis into its next generation of compounds.

The drug design methodology consists of iterative cycles of design, simulation, synthesis, structural assessment, and redesign. The pharmaceutical industry tries to adapt design rules known from the machinery industry to the far more complex world of molecules.

Conclusions

Since its establishment, the pharmaceutical industry has always been one of the most research-intensive and innovative sectors of manufacturing. The most recent scientific and technological revolution in the pharmaceutical industry initially started in the late 1970s and early 1980s with the rise of the biotechnology industry. By now, ever more complex sciences and technologies meant to discover lead substances are being used in pharmaceutical R&D, such as high-throughput screening, combinatorial chemistry, genomics-based technologies, proteomics or rational drug design. The novelty, complexity and strategic impact of these sciences and technologies on the industry and society have led to the general opinion that a new third industrial revolution has begun.

Due to the high complexity of these novel sciences and technologies, no single pharmaceutical company alone will be able to cope with the challenges imposed by these developments. The increasing pressure to gain access to these technologies forces pharmaceutical companies to open their boundaries and look beyond their own research borders. The case of Merck, which contributes just about 1% of worldwide biomedical research and is looking for ways to access the remaining 99%, is just one example that illustrates what the future landscape in pharmaceutical R&D will look like: Collaborations with universities, research institutions, biotechnology and genomics-based companies will significantly increase. Only the pharmaceutical companies that are able to manage these cooperations optimally will most likely be capable to introduce innovative products successfully on the market.

IV. The Pipeline Management Challenge: How to Shape the Innovation-Flow

> *„Pharmaceutical companies can best create value by finding a flow of innovative medicines that answer the needs of doctors and their patients. The companies that will succeed in the long term are the ones that best sustain this flow. "*
>
> Fred Hassan,
> then CEO at Pharmacia, 2002

The Importance of Pipeline Management

At any given time there are more than 1'000 drugs in development (PhRMA 2001). In 2000, the breakdown was as follows: more than 100 for AIDS, 350 for cancer, 120 for heart diseases and strokes, 26 for Alzheimer's disease, 25 for diabetes, and more than 200 for special needs of children. In order to maintain or exceed double-digit growth expectations, pharmaceutical companies are required to deliver between two and four new drugs every year. Given the high attrition rate in drug development, they have to fill the R&D pipeline with as many new drug candidates as possible.

According to Reuters (2003a), however, the pharmaceutical industry is suffering from a lack of genuine innovation. In many cases, pharmaceutical companies rely more on patent protection of existing drugs than on the invention of new drugs. Ironically, over-reliance on patents (intended to encourage investment in innovation) is reducing R&D productivity by diverting attention towards protecting existing product revenues from generic competition. This is a successful short-term strategy, given the relatively low costs of post-patent expiration competition vis-à-vis the huge investments required to develop a new molecular entity. But patent defense generates only incremental revenue compared to the potentially huge gains from new innovative products, and it creates an over-reliance on in-licensing to fill long-term revenue gaps.

Relying on blockbusters to drive the required sales growth, irrespective of company size, is an accepted practice provided there is sufficient depth in the pipeline to continually replace revenues lost to generic competition. However, historical analysis of the blockbuster market in 2000 by Reuters (2003a) suggests that this growth strategy has its weaknesses (see page 6). As mentioned earlier, the revenue forecast of year 2000 blockbuster drugs through to 2008 indicates that there will be an overall 3.8% decline in blockbuster sales over this period. Hence, companies can no longer simply rely on blockbuster products alone to drive double-digit revenue growth.

Pharmaceutical companies will have to compensate for declining block-buster growth by other means. In a first step, however, they have started to raise the investor community's attention to this trend. GlaxoSmithKline and Novartis have issued warnings not to underestimate the significance of declining blockbuster sales, given that the industry suffers from weak late-stage pipelines and new chemical entities have become increasingly diffi-cult to find.

However, sustaining the sales and, ideally, sales growth of blockbuster drugs throughout the lifecycle is necessary to optimize returns on R&D in-vestment and, in the absence of new products with blockbuster potential in the late stage pipeline, to fill gaps in a company's revenue stream.

The commercial strategy traditionally favored by large pharmaceutical companies – reflecting the belief that 'large markets equate to large reve-nues' – seems to have changed. Some biotechnology companies, for ex-ample, successfully pursue a different development strategy and target niche indications. What was generally considered an inefficient and low profit strategy may have turned into a high revenue strategy. Amgen's blockbuster Epogen, primarily used to treat anemia associated with renal disease, has proven that an ability to address a high level of unmet need in a single prominent secondary clinical complication can offer significant growth opportunities (Reuters 2003a).

The major threats that all drugs on the market face as they transfer from the growth into the maturity and decline phases of their lifecycles include:

- The introduction of next generation products offering improved clinical efficacy and less side effects (i.e., a better toxicity profile);
- The launch of generic competition following patent expiry;
- The entrance of competitively priced newer products offering similar clinical benefits.

Different strategies exist that allow pharmaceutical companies to protect their drugs on the market. Popularity over a prolonged period of time, for example, can be maintained by continuously improving a product through reformulations and line extensions. Furthermore, the continued high investment in drug promotion could be another approach to extend revenue streams.

In addition, the emergence of new drug discovery technologies, such as genomics, pharmacogenomics and proteomics, has heralded new opportunities for the pharmaceutical industry to generate products of higher and more selective efficacy. Given the prospective individualization and mass customization in the pharmaceutical industry, concern arises that the era of blockbuster drugs has come to an end. R&D investment is increasingly focused on using genomics and its associated technologies to target smaller patient populations with specific genotypes and, therefore, inherent tendencies towards certain medical conditions. Hence, it is justified to ask whether the mass application of a single drug to a large patient population will remain a viable strategy for the future.

However, there is an emerging belief that pharmacogenomics-derived products will not mean the end of the blockbuster paradigm; rather, they will help change the accepted definition of these high earning products to that of 'multi-busters', a series of personalized therapies that are able to dominate a certain targeted disease area. According to Reuters (2003a), these products will not present a threat to the blockbuster market because:

- Current blockbusters successfully treating a broad range of patients will not be targeted by post-genomic technologies unless they can sustain a product's market presence in the face of increasing competition.
- Post-genomic technologies will enable companies to build disease market franchises that address the different genotype profiles within target patient groups.
- Pharmaceutical companies will pursue a dual strategy of genomics-based diagnostic/therapeutic disease management. This will lower overall costs of future healthcare and justify higher drug prices.

Novartis' Gleevec: How can genomics-based drugs target micro-segmented markets?

Novartis' Gleevec is a good example of a currently marketed product that illustrates how markets may become micro-segmented under a genomics-driven business model (see Reuters 2003a). Gleevec has blockbuster potential but, unlike mass-market megadrugs, it targets a small group of patients and medical specialists. On 10 May 2001, Gleevec received FDA approval for the treatment of patients with chronic myelogenous leukemia (CML). By then, Gleevec had already become a market leader for the treatment of CML primarily because of its ability to target a chromosomal abnormality that occurs in only a small segment of the population. Historically, chronic leukemia has not been the focus of significant R&D investment because of the disease's prominence among the frail elderly who cannot tolerate chemotherapy, and because of its relatively low incidence and prevalence. The market for drugs launched for this indication was not considered sufficient in size to allow companies to recoup their R&D investment. Accordingly, only a handful of drugs have been approved for chronic leukemia in the last decade, the majority of which had originally been developed for other indications or rapidly acquired additional, more-lucrative indications following launch.

Gleevec has generated lucrative revenues since its launch in 2001. Its success partly reflects Novartis' aggressive, pre-launch PR strategy to drive rapid sales growth in an emerging market. This made Gleevec the third most successful pharmaceutical launch in 2001. Novartis successfully exploited the Internet to generate extensive pre-launch awareness of Gleevec and its benefits among patients, which ultimately led to a large surge in demand for the drug immediately upon launch. While Gleevec was still in early phase clinical trials, a US patient became so excited about the drug's trial results that she convinced more than 3'000 other patients and care givers to sign a letter to Novartis' CEO requesting that clinical trials be accelerated. Global 'e-word-of-mouth' spread quickly and Novartis had to mobilize consumer targeted PR to respond to patients' concerns. In the end, during the launch of Gleevec, Novartis' sales representatives were surprised to find leukemia patients in their training rooms who had been cured by Gleevec. These patients told the sales reps their personal stories about how Gleevec saved their lives.

The Complexity of Drug Discovery

A research study by Reuters (2002) applied an 'innovation index' to different companies from different industries in order to analyze their relative effectiveness in delivering innovation. A cross-industry comparison allowed to benchmark the pharmaceutical industry against other industries. According to this benchmark, the pharmaceutical industry is ranked worldwide as only the sixth most effective industry in generating innovation, behind aerospace and defense, automotive, electrical/electronics, chemicals and IT hardware. The average pharmaceutical company, however, is almost twice as effective at delivering innovation as the average software and IT services company.

Compared to other industries, the innovation process in the pharmaceutical industry has some very special characteristics, most notably the regulatory environment, which has a direct impact on development time and marketing opportunities, as well as the very high risk during the development. In the past, only 1 of 5'000 product ideas on average was eventually launched on the market (Pfeiffer 2000), and only 1 out of 10'000 substances was used to become a marketable product (Völker 2001). However, as new screening technologies are increasingly being used, this ratio has improved significantly. Today, more than 100'000 substances can simultaneously be screened with relatively little effort. Modern information technology has dramatically increased efficiency and effectiveness in the early pharmaceutical innovation phase.

However, only three out of 10 drugs generate revenues that meet or exceed average R&D costs, and 20% of products with the highest returns generate 70% of total returns (according to a study by Duke University economists cited in Reuters, 2002). While in most industries the decision to terminate a project is made based on economic considerations, the typical reasons in the pharmaceutical industry are primarily scientific or technical ones.

The average time from initial idea to market is in the region of 13 years (see page 4). Thus, four out of five researchers retire or move on before they see any commercial impact of their work. This makes incentive systems and motivation a very complicated management issue in pharmaceutical R&D.

Given the obstacles for future R&D performance and productivity, the entire drug discovery process is confronted with structural challenges. Due to the unusually long development period, the effective patent protection of a drug in the market is very short. Some countries have therefore extended patent protection for pharmaceutical products by several years.

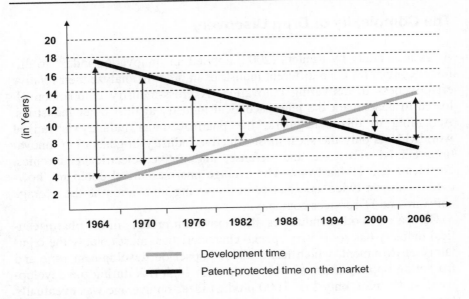

Development time
Patent-protected time on the market

Source: BPI (1999)

Fig. 29. The innovation scissors in the pharmaceutical industry.

Nevertheless, the trend towards longer development times means an even smaller window to recoup the investments (currently about 7-8 years compared to more then 17 years in the early 1960s). This phenomenon is referred to as the 'innovation scissors' in the pharmaceutical industry (see Fig. 29).

The primary reason for the long development time is the fact that failures are mostly becoming visible at later stages of the development process (e.g., during the clinical trials). While this pattern significantly extends the average development time, the primary objective for improvements in the drug discovery process should be to fail earlier in order to succeed sooner.

The drug discovery process is very complex and includes many different aspects – both managerial and technological – and covers several basic scientific disciplines, such as biology and chemistry (see Fig. 30).

Molecular biology, for example, takes on a particularly important role during the drug discovery process. It contributes to the understanding of the drug target function for onset, progression and chronicity of the disease. The validation of the drug target is key for the quality of lead identification. Hence, molecular biology allows for the development of recombinant molecules into a new molecular entity using a more rational approach. Mechanistic platforms for multigene-families and signal trans-

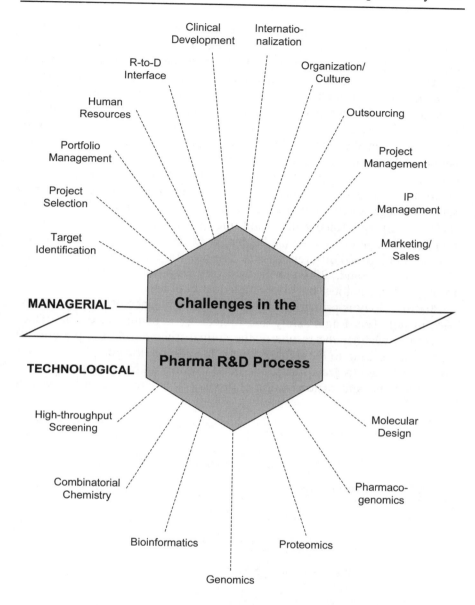

Fig. 30. Challenging aspects in the pharmaceutical R&D process.

duction pathways across disease areas can be established. More complex diseases increasingly require more complex therapeutic concepts and drugs. Sometimes, even a single compound can create its own market.

In chemistry (the primary source of new molecular entities) a shift towards more fundamental science has been observed. Researchers are trying to isolate as many compounds as possible from microorganisms, plants, fungi and marine organisms for new lead identification. The increasing rate of structural complexity can be handled by complementing experiments with computer simulations. Interactions of drug molecules with proteins can be visualized and databases can be used to analyze genes. New database technologies and improved statistical analyses are being used to manage the huge amounts of data. One single lab can produce more than 100 gigabytes of data per day. Hence, the primary goal in chemistry is to deliver as much input information as possible in order to screen through a sufficient amount of data to discover new substances. Simultaneously and equally important, the quality of the compound collection should be improved. At the beginning of 2003, all drugs on the market only hit in total 120 different targets. The top 100 drugs hit only 43 targets (Zambrowicz, Sands 2003). It is thus very important to screen not only through a large number but also a high quality of data.

Pharmacology is primarily coping with the relevance of the applied disease model. The drug's safety and toxicology is being tested. The major concern is whether the results of the animal trials during the pre-clinical studies are leading to the right products. In addition, the complexity of this task is expected to grow due to the trend towards an increasing segmentation of patients and customization of products to address individual patient

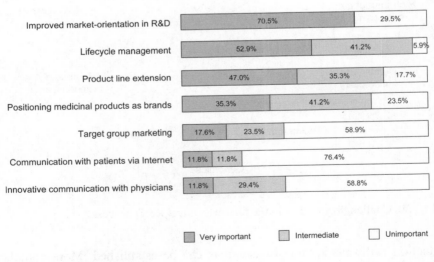

Source: Homburg & Partner (2001)

Fig. 31. Major marketing tasks for pharmaceutical companies.

profiles.

Marketing and sales are becoming increasingly important during the drug discovery process. A survey conducted by Homburg & Partner in collaboration with the University of Mannheim reveals that a market-orientation in pharmaceutical R&D is the foremost marketing task in the future (Fig. 31). However, the work of scientists today forms the basis for the industry in 20 years from now. Thus, the length of the innovation cycle makes it very difficult to gain the scientists' interest in today's commercial situation.

The same study by Homburg & Partner determined that the main driver for an improved customer-orientation is the increasing demand for information by the end-customers. The patients are requesting to become an equal partner in the entire health dialogue. Hence, a shift from a product-to a patient-driven strategy is necessary.

The Different Phases of the R&D Process

While the separation of the innovation process into research/pre-project and development phases significantly increases transparency and reduces costs in the main development phase (Albers, Eggers 1991), the introduction of the product into the market is often insufficiently considered. Despite their different management requirements, many companies do not distinguish between these different phases in R&D projects. For instance, Compaq has been making this distinction since 1987. It took a cross-functional team two years to define the specifications for a new personal computer during the pre-project phase. But this extended preparatory work allowed it to reduce the cost-intensive development phase to nine months.

Highly differentiated phase concepts are commonly accepted and applied in pharmaceutical R&D. The strictly sequential execution of project phases is sometimes considered impractical, but a given sine-qua-non in medical innovation. Projects must be carried out with reviews and milestones, not only to ensure drug candidate quality but also to document good laboratory practice. Only once the drug candidate is approved it is possible for the cost-intensive development phase to use structured engineering methods.

After the spectacular success of the Manhattan and Apollo projects, most companies have concentrated their R&D management efforts on project management. Today we know, at least in principle, how projects work. But we still do not know how to get from the many useful ideas to the vital few projects that an R&D lab is reasonably capable of executing.

Even more difficulties arise when the new product is to be introduced on the market. It is therefore suitable to distinguish three phases in the R&D process:

- Pre-project phase: How to create a good product concept and a manageable project
- Development phase: How to manage a project
- Market introduction: How to transfer R&D results efficiently to operations and the customer

The three phases are completely different (see Table 12). Translation of ideas and information is required at each interface. A different language dominates in each phase: the language of science, the language of the company, and the language of the customer. For instance, between the project and the market-introduction phases, we need to translate from the company's technical language to the oftentimes more emotion-based language of the sales force and the customer.

Table 12. Differences between pre-project, development, and market introduction phase.

Criteria	Pre-project Phase	Development Phase	Market Introduction Phase
Budget	Often none / low	Planned / medium	Planned / high
Goals	Vague	Detailed	Specified
Costs	Low	High	High
Processes	Not structured	Structured	Predetermined
Results	Unclear	Defined	Negotiated
Financial risk	Small	Medium	High

The three phases differ also from the international viewpoint. The pre-clinical phase can be quite low-key, simmering for years without well-defined structures and strongly dependent on individuals communicating face-to-face to stimulate creativity. The development phase focuses on efficient project execution. The plans and schedules developed in the pre-project phase are carried out. Work packages are allocated like modules to the best-suited teams wherever they are located in the world. There is tight networking within the group and efficient coordination at the higher level of project management, and at the inter-group level. Discipline is most important. The third phase of market-introduction is the truly international one: Teams are dispersed all over the world. They belong to different entities, perhaps meeting once a year and maintaining different goals. Negotiating is the name of the game. Tight project management is recommended, but only few companies apply it.

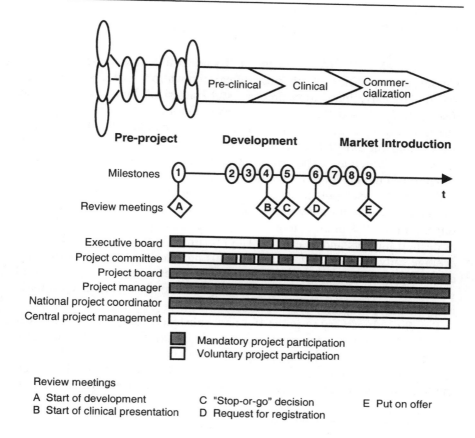

Fig. 32. The R&D process at Bayer.

BASF underscores the distinction between the pre-project and development phases by speaking of R&D 'activities' in the early R&D stages, and R&D 'projects' in later stages. Bayer requires that milestones and project review meetings must not take place before entering the pre-clinical phase when the project is formally started (Fig. 32).

Organizationally, companies renown as innovation leaders in pharmaceutical R&D have typically small, focused research organizations centered on core technologies and therapeutic competencies (Reuters 2002). This approach seems to be the most promising way to deliver effective R&D results.

The R&D Process at Hoffmann-La Roche

Let us consider the R&D process of Roche to illustrate some of the dynamics and qualities of pharmaceutical innovation (see also Borgulya 2000). The early innovation process is characterized by the research and discovery phase and the pre-clinical trials. During the research stage, the research project is defined and basic research is conducted. The scientists are looking for existing molecules, which could serve as a target for new substances, which are expected to have an impact on the disease which is about to be cured (Fig. 33).

During the screening stage, scientists look for a so-called lead-substance, which influences the target in the desired way. During this stage, almost 90% of all potential substances are eliminated due to the lack of desired impacts and/or effects. The remaining substances, which are on average only the few dozen most promising ones, are tested in the pre-clinical trials (Fig. 34). However, due to advancements in computer-based screening technologies, this number might have decreased substantially over the past few years.

Pre-clinical tests try to prove if a new substance takes effect and if it is compliant. The most important issues are to ensure that the new substance is not toxic, does not change genes and does not cause cancer or birth defects. This test-series is usually made using animal experiments. However, the total amount of animal experiments in Switzerland has decreased dra-

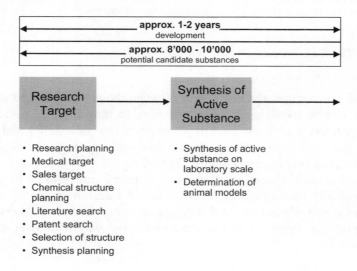

Fig. 33. Research concept and discovery of active substance at Roche.

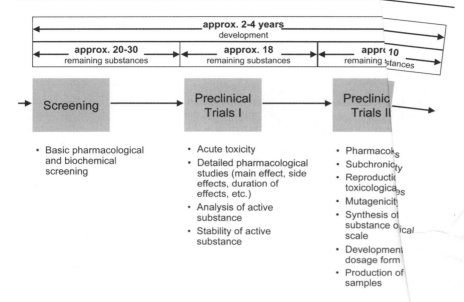

Fig. 34. Pre-clinical development at Roche.

matically from 2 million in 1983 to less than half a million in 1999, ;h
is a drop of 78%. Every animal experiment in Switzerland has to be _i-
cially approved by the Federal Office for Veterinarian Affairs. In cas_e
pre-clinical trials are successful, the substance is analyzed regarding
registration for the human being during the clinical trials (Fig. 35).

The clinical trials are separated into three different phases. During ph.
I, the drug candidate is tested whether its positive animal properties can
extended to humans (compatibility). 20-80 healthy volunteers are used
determine safety and dosage of the drug candidate. This phase can last u
to two years. During phase II, the substance is applied to about 100-30(
patients as well as to animals. The testing is done to see if the substance is
able to cure the disease. During phase III, the substance is being tried at a
larger number of patients in order to establish the proper dosage and any
adverse reactions to long-term use.

The average number of patients needed for new drug applications has
risen from about 1'500 in the late 1970s to about 4'500 in the mid-1990s
(PhRMA 1999). Novartis, for instance, included 14'000 patients in the
clinical studies of one of their most recent new drugs, which was introduced in the market in mid-2003. The primary rationale behind this large
sample were marketing reasons (i.e., to prove the drug's differentiation

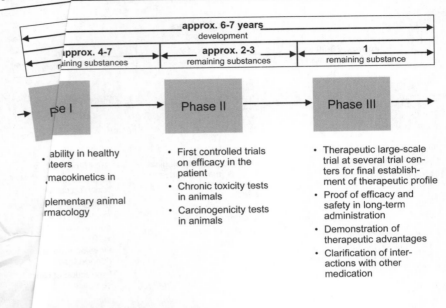

approx. 6-7 years
development

approx. 4-7
remaining substances

approx. 2-3
remaining substances

1
remaining substance

Phase I

Phase II

Phase III

- ability in healthy
  teers
- macokinetics in
- plementary animal
  rmacology

- First controlled trials on efficacy in the patient
- Chronic toxicity tests in animals
- Carcinogenicity tests in animals

- Therapeutic large-scale trial at several trial centers for final establishment of therapeutic profile
- Proof of efficacy and safety in long-term administration
- Demonstration of therapeutic advantages
- Clarification of interactions with other medication

5. Clinical development at Roche.

other products). In general, the purpose and the number of patients ing the clinical trials varies depending on the disease area. For example, cer drugs need different clinical trial sets than blood pressure drugs.

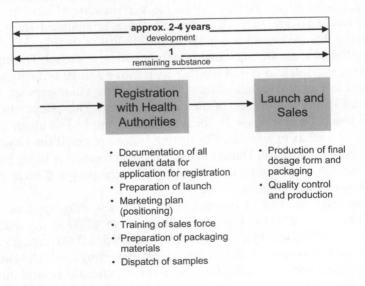

approx. 2-4 years
development

1
remaining substance

Registration with Health Authorities

Launch and Sales

- Documentation of all relevant data for application for registration
- Preparation of launch
- Marketing plan (positioning)
- Training of sales force
- Preparation of packaging materials
- Dispatch of samples

- Production of final dosage form and packaging
- Quality control and production

Fig. 36. Registration, launch and sales at Roche.

If the clinical trials are successful, the new product can be registered with the respective health authorities. After the registration, the new drug can finally be launched on the market accompanied by support from the sales force, and some potentially occurring additional side-effects need to be taken into consideration (see Fig. 36).

Conclusions

The drug development pipeline is the engine that drives pharmaceutical companies. Market valuations of pharmaceutical companies are based on prospected new drug approvals and expected new drug revenues. What is feeding these new approvals is a healthy and steady discovery of new drug candidates. Given the inherently uncertain nature of research, pharmaceutical companies are introducing new technologies to widen the intake of new drug candidates (as described in chapter 3) and new management methods and techniques to make drug development more efficient (as seen in this chapter). In the following chapter we will describe how pharmaceutical companies are branching out to cooperate with suppliers of information, technology, and customers, by outsourcing some steps in the pharmaceutical value chain or by internationalizing their R&D and innovative activities.

V. The Outsourcing and Internationalization Challenge: How to Harness Outside Innovation

Impact of Outsourcing on the Pharmaceutical Value Chain

A market survey by Arthur D. Little and Solvias (2002) has shown that only lead finding, lead optimization and marketing are seen as core activities of pharmaceutical companies that have to be provided 100% in-house. All other activities are potential candidates for outsourcing, except for project management, which is a backbone process ensuring efficient know-how transfer between the different steps in pharmaceutical innovation. In fact, this outsourcing potential could have a major impact on the pharmaceutical value chain (Fig. 37).

Although outsourcing is controversially discussed in the pharmaceutical industry due to the high complexity in drug discovery, outsourcing some R&D activities to pharmaceutical service providers might lead to time and cost savings, would allow for access to new technologies and know-how and could help manage peak resource shortages. Many pharmaceutical companies already work with multiple outsourcing partners during the innovation process to build greater experience in managing value networks rather than just value chains. Besides biotechnology, genomics-based and other platform companies, these partners include a wide variety of contract service organizations (CSOs). The term CSO includes contract research organizations (CRO), contract manufacturing organizations (CMO), site management organizations (SMO), and any other organization that provides pharmaceutical companies with a contract service. Research by Lehman Brothers (1999) has shown that contract research organizations are able to conduct clinical trials up to 30% faster than the average large pharmaceutical company. In 1999, pharmaceutical companies spent about 25% of their R&D budgets for services provided by CROs. This number is expected to increase to about 40% (see Lehman Brothers 1999). At this stage, the CRO industry consists of over 1'000 companies based in the US,

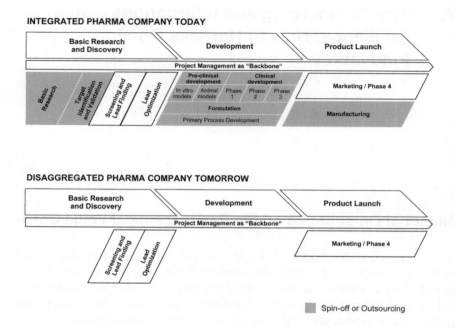

Fig. 37. Impact of outsourcing on the pharmaceutical value chain according to Arthur D. Little.

Europe and Asia. There are many rather small CROs which usually are regionally embedded into local market structures.

The entire market for pharmaceutical R&D outsourcing was US$ 9.3 billion in 2001 and is predicted to reach US$ 36 billion by 2010. This represents an annual growth rate of 16.3% compared to an average expected growth in global R&D expenditure of 9.6% during the same period (Reuters 2003c). Most of this outsourced effort is being expended on non-clinical drug development, clinical trials, and manufacturing aspects of the drug development process.

Outsourcing requires the pharmaceutical company to think and act in a more process-oriented way. Barriers between intra-organizational units as well as to external partners are expected to diminish. External experts could either be integrated into the innovation process for a limited time or they could just provide some necessary infrastructure and basic services to the pharmaceutical company. Primary drivers for outsourcing include:

- Reduction of over-capacities (as a result of M&A activity);
- Cost cutting or restructuring issues;

- Growth aspirations (expertise, resources);
- Reduction of risk and/or proactive risk management;
- Corporate governance and/or strategic make-or-by decision.

The final decision to outsource R&D functions usually depends on many different parameters (see also Festel, Polastro 2002):

- Technological requirements and specifications (technologies and synthesis techniques, available capacities, status of registration);
- Product-specific considerations (quantity, position within the lifecycle, impact on the overall product portfolio);
- Financial aspects (investments, economic feasibility: in-house production vs. outsourced production);
- Taxes (the access to medical substances is oftentimes used in order to optimize the tax load);
- Market access (despite new developments, the pharmaceutical industry is still characterized by a more or less open protectionism);
- 'Chemical' tradition of the pharmaceutical company (philosophy, commitment to chemical processes).

If a pharmaceutical company intends to outsource some part of its R&D activities to an external service provider, three questions are important (see Arthur D. Little, Solvias 2002):

- What kind of services could potentially be interesting for R&D outsourcing?
- What are the most effective and efficient interfaces between the pharmaceutical company and the service provider?
- Which cooperation models are the best basis for managing the outsourcing activities?

The kind of activities that could be outsourced to service providers is usually dependant upon the characteristics of the pharmaceutical company. It has been shown that big pharmaceutical companies, mid-size pharmaceutical companies and start-ups usually adopt different outsourcing strategies.

Big pharmaceutical companies are typically involved in outsourcing activities for strategic reasons. In the early phases, this includes such things as process development, scale-up and delivery of first lot sizes for clinical trials. The goal is to circumvent bottlenecks in one's own development process and to manage peak resource shortages. Mid-size pharmaceutical companies usually concentrate on one or two products emanating from their own R&D pipeline. While outsourcing structures of mid-size pharmaceutical companies are typically comparable to big pharmaceutical

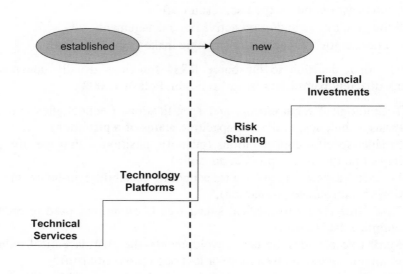

Fig. 38. Objects for outsourcing.

companies, the major difference is the low proportion of outsourced sub-stances of older compounds. Hence, the focus of contract-synthesis lies more on advanced intermediate products rather than on substances. Start-ups, as the third type of pharmaceutical companies, are typically very much characterized by limited capacities in synthesis development and production. As a result, they could almost entirely have to rely on outsourcing and, hence, represent a huge market for pharmaceutical ser-vice providers. However, the service provider always has to consider the significant risk during the development process.

Besides outsourcing relatively straight-forward activities such as devel-opment services or the management of technology platforms, the pharma-ceutical company could proactively use service providers to outsource even more complex tasks (Fig. 38).

Novel objects for outsourcing could include that the service provider helps share drug development risks. Furthermore, the pharmaceutical company itself could actively support outsourcing activities by making fi-nancial investments into legal entities that serve as an outsourcing partner. A good example for the latter case is the Novartis Venture Fund which provides capital for spin-offs in order to reduce non-needed capacities and release entrepreneurial responsibility and capability.

Novartis Venture Fund

The Novartis Venture Fund was founded in 1996 and supports new business projects that show entrepreneurial spirit in the health science areas. In 2002, Novartis increased the amount of capital in the Novartis Venture Fund with an additional grant of CHF 50 million. This brings the total fund size to about CHF 300 million. Since the Funds' inception, 117 companies were funded, and 68 companies have been part of the equity portfolio at the end of 2002. The entire fund is comprised of three different funds: the Spin-off Fund, the Start-up Fund, and the BioVenture Fund.

The mission of the Spin-off Fund is to support, coach and facilitate Novartis spin-offs on a worldwide basis. In most cases the Fund provides seed money to support employees who want to create their own business, based on a convincing business plan. The Start-up Fund supports entrepreneurship and investments in start-up companies mainly from European universities. The Fund offers seed money, but frequently assists the companies throughout further financing rounds. The objective of the BioVenture Fund is to invest in product- and platform-focused biotechnology, pharmaceutical and healthcare companies at all stages, with an emphasis on the United States.

The Novartis Venture Fund supports companies worldwide, for example in Switzerland, the US, and Singapore. In Novartis' hometown Basel alone, the Novartis Venture Fund has helped establish 42 companies which so far generated combined annual revenues of about CHF 90 million and created almost 700 jobs.

Successful Commercialization of a Breakthrough Technology

As an illustration of a partnership between two companies to exploit the full potential of a new technology, the following case describes the commercialization of InnoGel™, a breakthrough soft capsule technology, and covers in detail the structure of the commercialization process*. The com-

---

* This case study was generously provided by Dr. Marc Müller, InterPharmaLink.

mercialization of InnoGel™ was performed through a joint collaboration between NovoGEL and InterPharmaLink.

The InnoGel™ technology has been developed by NovoGEL, a spin-off company, which holds all rights to the InnoGel™ technology and acts as a licensor towards interested parties.

InterPharmaLink is a specialized healthcare management consulting firm that has the exclusive and worldwide mandate to commercialize the InnoGel™ technology. InterPharmaLink helps their clients optimize key resources along the value chain and create value added through product portfolio optimization, supply chain optimization and business development.

Soft capsule market

About 100 billion soft capsules are produced throughout the world per year. Virtually all of this volume is manufactured by contract manufacturers and accounts for a market of about US$ 1.5 billion. Soft capsules are mainly applied in the industries of pharmaceuticals, health and nutrition, and cosmetics. The soft capsule market is dominated by two contract manufacturers: R.P. Scherer, the originator of the rotary die soft capsule manufacturing process and Banner Pharmacaps. The rest of the soft capsule market is served by several other companies.

Soft capsules are a means of packaging whereby the capsule content is encapsulated by a shell. The state of the art technology for the soft capsule shell is gelatin. The development of a non-animal alternative to gelatin has been a top priority in the soft capsule industry for many years. Several attempts to replace gelatin by non-animal material have been made already. But none of them have been overly successful. The InnoGel™ technology is a starch based gelatin replacement technology which has the clear potential to revolutionize the soft capsule market as it offers truly unique material properties and significant cost advantages versus gelatin.

InnoGel™ technology

The InnoGel™ technology is based on starch gel, an ordered material with a partly crystalline network structure. The network density can be adjusted by varying the composition and the physical treatment of the starch gel. It is the unique feature of the network structure that has lead experts to believe that the InnoGel™ technology can produce soft capsules for health and nutritional as well as for pharmaceutical products that offer major improvements to available technologies. These improvements manifest themselves in various strategic and financial benefits:

- Additional market potential due to suitability for vegetarians and cultures averse to animal sources (bovine or porcine);
- Increased value proposition vs. customers due to superior capsule properties and suitability as a lifecycle management tool for pharmaceutical products;
- Improved safety for end-users and reduced risk profile for customers due to elimination of BSE risks;
- Significantly lower raw material cost due to lower price of starch versus gelatin;
- Significantly lower process cost due to higher yield, less rejections, shorter process time, lower energy consumption and easier handling;
- Significantly lower packaging and logistic cost due to superior capsule properties.

Commercialization process

The aspiration of the commercialization is to capture a maximum share of the value creation potential of the InnoGel™ technology. Thus, the successful commercialization of the InnoGel™ technology is performed along a clearly defined process. The commercialization process is structured in three major process steps:

Step 1: Define the basic conditions of the commercialization;
Step 2: Develop the strategy of the commercialization;
Step 3: Manage the licensing-out process.

Basic conditions of the commercialization

At the beginning, NovoGEL and InterPharmaLink agreed on the important conditions of the commercialization of the InnoGel™ technology with regard to confidentiality, timing and financials:

- Only non-confidential information could be disclosed to interested parties as the patent application is only published four months after the project starts.
- Only very limited financial and personal resources could be applied to the commercialization of InnoGel™, as NovoGEL is a start-up company with only limited financial capabilities.

- The first license should be granted within twelve months after project start in order to ensure the financial stability and future projects of NovoGEL.

In addition, both parties agreed on a collaboration agreement with clear incentives for both parties to fully exploit the value creation potential of the InnoGel™ technology and to perform the commercialization process in best time and at lowest cost.

Strategy of the commercialization

The goal of the strategic planning of commercialization is to fully exploit the value creation potential of the InnoGel™ technology while considering the given conditions (i.e., tight schedule of commercialization and limited applicable resources). A successful commercialization strategy is based on a thorough analysis of the strategic landscape and addresses the strategic questions of where, how and when to compete.

The major soft capsule manufacturers were identified as the primary target group for commercialization. These contract manufacturers possess an extensive know-how and long-term experience in soft capsule manufacturing and have virtually all necessary equipment available to perform the technical evaluation, as well as the subsequent application development in best time. The most important selling arguments for contract manufacturers are cost saving potentials on the raw materials, as well as strategic aspects regarding BSE risks and issues. The soft capsule manufacturing process is mainly operated by contract manufacturers serving companies in the pharmaceutical, health and nutrition or cosmetics industry.

Thus, companies with considerable capsule volumes wanting to reduce or eliminate their dependency on contract manufacturers by re-integrating the soft capsule manufacturing into their in-house production facilities, have been evaluated as secondary target group.

The licensing-out of the InnoGel™ technology has been identified as the most promising approach for commercialization. As the InnoGel™ technology is still in the development stages and the future licensee will have to perform further development activities, a combined technical evaluation and option for licensing agreement is considered the most appropriate alternative. In order to ensure maximum know-how protection for licensee and licensor and preserve the exclusivity of the know-how, the licensing-out is done along the lines of a structured bidding process among interested parties.

The timeline of commercialization is set at the beginning of the project, meaning the first license should be granted within twelve months after project start. This early decision was mainly driven by the aspirations of the NovoGEL business plan.

Without these given constraints, a detailed assessment of the impact of the timeline on the exploitation of the value creation potential would have been the appropriate way to proceed. With an immediate commercialization the value creation potential for NovoGEL is clearly limited, as the InnoGel™ technology is an early development stage project with unproved realization guarantee. On the other hand, the risks for NovoGEL are clearly limited as well because the complete application development will be performed by the future licensee.

Licensing-out process

In order to further develop and commercialize the InnoGel™ technology in a way that gives maximum protection of know-how to licensee and licensor, the licensing-out of InnoGel™ is done along the lines of a structured bidding process among the top global soft capsule manufacturers. The exclusive rights granted consist of the rights to perform an exclusive technical evaluation coupled with an option for subsequent licensing. In order to preserve the exclusivity of the know-how, the commercialization process incorporates the following basic principles:

- The exclusive technical evaluation is linked with the option for licensing. Therefore, the future licensee will have to sign a combined technical evaluation and option for licensing agreement prior to starting the exclusive technical evaluation phase.
- The detailed know-how for the exclusive technical evaluation (e.g., the recipe of the starch gel), as well as the process parameters will only be provided to the party signing the combined technical evaluation and option for licensing agreement.

The technical evaluation and option for licensing agreement incorporates the conditions of the exclusive technical evaluation phase as well as the conditions of a subsequent licensing agreement. Interested parties are offered the following conditions for an exclusive technical evaluation phase and subsequent licensing:

- The exclusive technical evaluation phase is limited to a three month period and is based on a detailed work plan describing the planned trials as well as the timelines to be met for the results. Both parties agree to 'target outcome results' in order to determine whether the technical evaluation is successful.

- Whether the technical evaluation is successful or not will be assessed by an independent committee on the basis of predetermined 'target outcome results'. Subsequently, the evaluating party has to decide whether it wants to exercise its option for licensing or not.
- All intellectual property rights and patents as well as results derived from activities during the technical evaluation phase shall belong to NovoGEL. In the case where the licensing option is exercised, the rights and results will be part of a subsequent license.

The decision with whom to enter into concrete negotiations to sign the combined technical evaluation and option for licensing agreement, is based on a set of qualitative and quantitative aspects; particularly the following aspects:

- What timeline can be agreed upon and what trials are to be performed during the technical evaluation period?
- What technical evaluation fee is offered when signing the combined technical evaluation and option for licensing agreement?
- What down payment and/or exit fee is offered? A down payment is payable if the technical evaluation is successful and the evaluating party wants to exercise the option for licensing. An exit fee is payable if the technical evaluation is successful and the evaluating party does not want to exercise the option for licensing.
- What first and second milestone payments are offered? A first milestone payment is payable when the first health and nutritional product is on the market. A second milestone payment is payable when the first pharmaceutical product achieves regulatory approval.
- What royalties are offered? Royalties are payable based on the number of InnoGel™ capsules sold.

The decision with whom to enter into negotiations for signing the combined technical evaluation, and the option for the licensing agreement, is based on the attractiveness of the offers submitted by interested parties.

Lessons learned

Lessons learned from the successful commercialization of InnoGel™ can be identified in the following three areas:

- Define the basic conditions and requirements of the commercialization with regard to timing and financials and set-up a detailed work plan;

- Analyze the market and develop a commercialization strategy that provides clear answers to the questions of where, how and when to compete and respect own resources;
- Set up a well structured licensing-out process that ensures the capture of a maximum share of the value of the technology for the licensor while preserving the exclusivity of know-how to the licensee. Conduct open and fair negotiations.

Trends and Drivers of Internationalization

As a science-driven endeavor, the pharmaceutical industry is inherently global. This is even more true for pharmaceutical companies originating in small countries, where high R&D costs can only be recouped by selling the resulting drug to a worldwide market. International trade statistics by the WTO (2002) illustrate the tremendous increase in international business over the past twenty years. For instance, the amount of worldwide merchandise exports has risen from about US$ 2 trillion to almost US$ 7 trillion between 1985 and 2000. Europe accounts for about 36% of the 2000 trade number (of which about 22% was intra-European trade), Asia about 28%, and the US about 12%. Among the big movers is Asia, which almost doubled its worldwide share from 16% in 1980. China went up from about 1% to now 4%, and Korea, also increased from 1% to 3%. Africa is one of the losers in this picture, dropping from 6% to 2% by 2000.

Although many smaller multinationals that previously relied on centralized R&D now engage in sourcing technology from around the world, R&D internationalization during the 1980s and 1990s was largely driven by multinational companies. The pioneers of R&D internationalization are high-tech companies operating in small markets and with little R&D resources in their home country, as it is the case for ABB, Novartis and Hoffmann-La Roche (Switzerland), Philips (Netherlands) or Ericsson (Sweden). Swiss, Dutch and Belgian companies carried out more than 50% of their R&D outside their home country by the end of the 1980s. These companies increasingly conducted R&D in foreign research laboratories. Companies such as General Electric and General Motors in the USA, Toyota and Fujitsu in Japan, and DaimlerChrysler in Germany had large home markets and a substantial domestic R&D base, and hence had less pressure to internationalize their R&D activities. Only in recent years has increased competition from within and outside their industries forced these companies to source technological knowledge on a global scale.

Although the trend towards R&D internationalization had become apparent in the 1970s, it became a widespread phenomenon only as recently as in the late 1980s (Cantwell 1995). In the mid-1990s, the fifty largest R&D spenders worldwide accounted for a considerable share of total R&D input in each of the triad nations (33% in the US, 42% in Western Europe, and 57% in Japan), thus highlighting the importance of (international) R&D activities carried out by multinational companies (Gassmann, von Zedtwitz 1999). The significance of international R&D activities is even greater when indirect influence of these companies on small- and medium-sized enterprises is taken into account.

As early as 1986, Dutch and Swiss companies had more laboratories outside their home countries than within (Pearce, Singh 1990). Between 1985 and 1993, overseas investment in R&D by US firms increased three times as fast as domestic R&D. In the US, overseas R&D expenses reached 10% of overall R&D investment, up from 6% in 1985 (National Science Board 1996). In the same period, the share of majority-owned foreign affiliates' R&D in the US rose from 9% to over 15% (National Science Board 1996). In 1991, Japanese multinational companies conducted less than 5% of their R&D abroad (Buderi et al. 1991), but the recent establishment of Japanese laboratories in Europe and the US has increased the significance of Japanese-based global R&D (see e.g., Dalton, Serapio 1995). By 1991, European companies performed about one third of their R&D outside of their home countries. More recent research shows that the trends of R&D internationalization in these three regions have been maintained (von Zedtwitz, Gassmann 2002).

The management of cross-border R&D activities is characterized by a significantly higher degree of complexity than local R&D management. The extra costs of international coordination must be balanced by synergy effects such as decreased time-to-market, improved effectiveness, and enhanced learning capabilities. Top corporate managers are confronted with the task of finding the optimal R&D organization based on the type of R&D activities, the present geographic dispersion of subsequent value-adding activities such as production and marketing, and the coordination between a multitude of contributors to the R&D process.

Nevertheless, the amount of international R&D activity is significant. Fig. 39 presents R&D investments of technology-intensive companies by rate of R&D internationalization and R&D-to-sales ratio. While many companies are still below 30% R&D internationalization, their total absolute overseas R&D investment is still very impressive given the large multiplier of their annual R&D budgets. Most highly internationalized R&D organizations are the results of merger and acquisition activity, as is the case for ABB, Royal Dutch/Shell, Mettler-Toledo, and others.

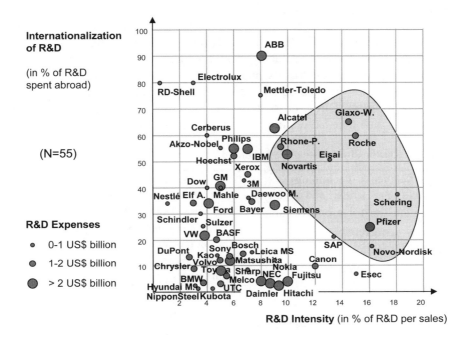

Fig. 39. Pharmaceutical firms have high degrees of R&D intensity and internationalization.

Pharmaceutical companies are characterized by a high R&D intensity (i.e., a high R&D-to-sales ratio). Many of the pharmaceutical companies included in Fig. 39 are in a variety of life science related businesses, and thus their R&D intensity increases even further (to an average of 20%) if sales only of ethical drugs are considered, which account for the lion's share of the R&D expenses. As pharmaceutical R&D is also relatively highly internationalized, most of the pharmaceutical firms are found in the top-right hand portion of the figure.

What drives R&D internationalization? Most factors are due to either science & technology-related issues or sales & output efficiency. Science & technology-related factors are concerned with R&D personnel qualification, know-how sourcing and regional infrastructure. These factors are largely outside the direct influence of R&D but necessary for its fundamental operations, such as the proximity to universities or the R&D environment. Proximity to markets and customers, improvements of image and collaborations are notable sales & output efficiency-related factors. Efficiency-related criteria focus on the costs of running and the critical mass of R&D units, as well as efficient hand-over processes between R&D and other corporate functions. Direct cost advantages (such as the often publicized labor costs) rarely influence the internationalization of R&D, but other efficiency-oriented factors such as costs of coordination and transfer, and critical laboratory size do have an even bigger impact on international R&D organization. Direct costs may become more important in the coming years as the other factors improve in low labor cost countries.

Table 13. Reasons for locating R&D abroad.

Science & Technology	Sales & Output Efficiency
Availability of scientists and engineers	Smooth hand-over with local marketing and sales organization
Tapping into local scientific community	
Proximity to universities	Easier coordination with local hospitals during the clinical phases
Recruiting local talent	
Better R&D environment	Compliance with local regulatory requirements
Higher quality of life	
Lower R&D costs	24-h-Laboratories
Higher acceptance for pharmaceutical research	'Good citizen' argument
	Local content rules
	Protectionist barriers
	Tax optimization

Political and socio-cultural factors such as local content rules, technology acceptance and public approval times, all play an important role in locating R&D abroad. Protectionist, legal and cultural constraints imposed by national governments, however, often require a company to establish local R&D units. R&D-external forces such as a business unit's striving for autonomy and the build-up of local competence alters the original mission of a local R&D unit. This evolution may take place unbeknownst to headquarters, particularly in strongly decentralized companies.

In the pharmaceutical industry, mergers and acquisitions have significantly contributed to the internationalization of R&D, particularly with recent cross-border mergers. Subsequent cost reduction programs eliminated R&D units in the combined company, but since both domestic and foreign units were closed down, this had little effect on their new extent of R&D internationalization. Rather, we observed a centralization of R&D in certain internationally leading regions of innovation (centers of excellence). However, mergers are rarely driven by scientific or technological reasons. Access to new markets and economies-of-scale effects are primary drivers for mergers. Nevertheless, the resulting R&D conglomerate has to live and cope with a new more international organization.

The development of local products requires the early involvement of market and customer application know-how, which is more likely to be found in regional business units. Companies with local R&D exhibit an inclination towards over-emphasizing different local market specification in order to support local autonomy and independence from the parent company. Host country restrictions, such as local content requirements, tolls, import quota, and fulfillment of standards, can attract R&D into key market countries (*pull regulations*). On the other hand, home country restrictions may induce companies to move R&D abroad (*push regulations*): European regulations caused biotechnology R&D to be transferred to the US. In addition, external factors have had a great impact on the dispersion of R&D sites.

The case for R&D internationalization is not unanimous. Besides the ubiquitous cost argument, foreign R&D units are more difficult to manage, and control, and may be less efficient due to missed scale effects. The following table summarizes some of the most cited arguments against international R&D.

Table 14. Barriers to R&D internationalization.

Factors in support of central R&D	Obstacles to international R&D
Economies of scale (critical size)	Immobility of top-class personnel
Synergy effects	Critical mass (for start-ups)
Higher career potential	Redundant development
Minimal R&D costs and development time	Language and cultural differences
	Effective communication difficult
Better control over research results	Much of scientific and technical information worldwide available by Internet
Communication intensity	
Legal protection	Specific know-how easily lost when support not present
Global product standards	
Common R&D culture	Political risks in target country
Harmonization of regulatory environment	Establishment and running costs
	No wage advantages in triad nations
Improved information and communication technologies	Coordination and information costs

R&D Internationalization of Swiss Pharmaceutical Companies

Switzerland as R&D location

Switzerland is an attractive location for research and development. Novartis, Roche and Serono invested approximately CHF 3.1 billion in pharmaceutical R&D in Switzerland in 2001, which is equivalent to 43.3% of their global R&D spending. The geographic concentration of the pharmaceutical industry in the northwest of Switzerland, its proximity to a large number of other small and mid-size companies in the broadly defined healthcare segment, and its proximity to very good research centers within universities are central reasons why Switzerland is an excellent pharmaceutical R&D location (creation of innovation clusters).

The increase in the number of small and mid-size biotechnology companies in Switzerland has become a significantly important factor. In general, the nature of biotechnology firms is to focus on research because they are still developing their initial products. Marketing and sales forces grow only when a viable product nears government approval. Hence, the 130 biotechnology firms in Switzerland represent a great pool of resources for R&D activities and highlight Switzerland's worldwide importance as an R&D location.

Besides the close interactions between biotechnology and pharmaceutical companies, Swiss science is among the most recognized regarding pharmaceutical fundamental research. The Swiss Scientific Council (Schweizer Wissenschaftsrat) compared fundamental research in Switzerland to other OECD countries. A citation-index providing information on how often scientific papers are quoted by other scientists (total number of quotes divided by number of publications) was calculated. The source of this research was a database of the Institute for Scientific Information (ISI, Philadelphia) from 1994 to 1998. About 5'000 scientific journals ranging from medicine and mathematics, 1'500 scientific journals about social sciences and another 1'100 journals from humanities and arts were included into the database. Table 15 illustrates the leading role of Switzerland in terms of the citation-index in 7 different disciplines.

As a result, research in Switzerland on new drug development seems to be quite successful. New drugs, which have been introduced on the Swiss market over the past few years, resulted to the following mortality reductions (VIPS 2002):

- The mortality of AIDS-patients between 1994 and 1999 by 93%;

Table 15. Fundamental research according to the OECD citation-index.

	Rank			
	1	2	3	4
Molecular Biology / Genetics	CH	USA	UK	FIN
Immunology	CH	USA	BEL	GER
Pharmacology	CH	AUS	UK	SWE
Chemistry	CH	USA	NL	NOR
Physics	CH	USA	NOR	FIN
Botany / Zoology	CH	UK	NL	USA
Ecology / Environmental Studies	CH	SWE	NL	USA
Biology / Biochemistry	USA	CH	GER	UK
Neuro Sciences	USA	CH	UK	GER
Microbiology	USA	BEL	CH	NL

Source: Swiss Scientific Council (1999)

- The mortality of prostate cancer patients between 1990 and 1996 by 17%, stomach cancer patients by 29%, colon cancer patients by 22%, cardiovascular patients by 13%, and heart patients by 11%;
- The two-year mortality between 1992 and 1995 after an attack of instable angina by 55%;
- The two-year mortality between 1992 and 1995 after a heart attack by 18%.

Pharmaceutical R&D spending in Switzerland

According to the Swiss Federal Office for Statistics (Bundesamt für Statistik), total expenditures for research and development activities within Switzerland were CHF 10'675 million in 2000. The private sector accounted for about 69%, the public authorities for 25% and other institutions for 6%.

Hence, the bulk of research and development expenditures is contributed by private organizations. According to Economiesuisse (2002), private R&D expenditures can be differentiated into intramuros expenditures, extramuros expenditures, and R&D expenditures of foreign subsidiaries of Swiss firms. While intramuros expenditures cover R&D expenses spent by a firm for its own R&D labs inside Switzerland, extramuros expenditures cover R&D jobs outsourced to third parties either within Switzerland or abroad.

The pharmaceutical-chemical industry accounted for CHF 2'475 million or 32% of intramuros expenditures as well as for CHF 905 million or 53%

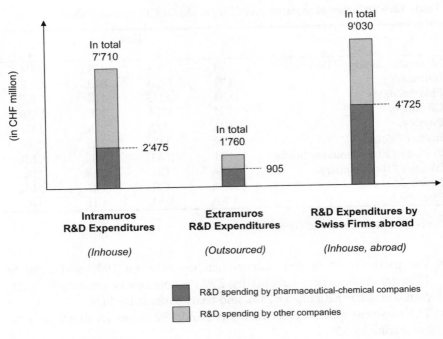

Source: Economiesuisse (2002)

Fig. 40. R&D spending by Swiss pharmaceutical-chemical companies in 2000.

of extramuros expenditures in 2000. Out of the CHF 905 million extra-muros expenditures, the pharmaceutical-chemical industry spent about 92% on research projects abroad compared with just 42% in 1996. Out of the CHF 9'030 million in R&D spending by Swiss companies abroad, the pharmaceutical-chemical industry covers 52% or CHF 4'725 million (Economiesuisse 2002). This further stresses the significant shift in R&D spending by Swiss pharmaceutical-chemical companies towards foreign subsidiaries.

Out of the CHF 2'475 million of total intramuros R&D spending in the pharmaceutical-chemical industry, about CHF 1'300 million was spent on experimental development, CHF 1'000 million on applied research and another CHF 200 million on fundamental research.

R&D spending in biotechnology increased to around CHF 300 million in 2000. Pharmaceutical-chemical companies as well as research laboratories accounted for 75% of this amount, which again highlights the close interactions between pharmaceutical firms and biotechnology firms.

Of 41'350 people working in R&D in Switzerland, the pharmaceutical-chemical industry employs 8'800 people or 21% of the total R&D workforce in Switzerland in 2000, this is compared to 11'360 or 30.4% in 1996. Hence, the pharmaceutical-chemical industry has been scaling down its R&D staff in Switzerland over the past years. About 36% of R&D employees in Switzerland have a college/university degree.

Of 8'800 people working in R&D in the pharmaceutical-chemical industry in Switzerland, about 45% are foreigners compared to an average of 33% of foreigners for all industries. Two-thirds (67%) of foreign employees working in the pharmaceutical-chemical industry in Switzerland hold a college/university degree.

R&D spending by Interpharma companies

The three Interpharma companies – Novartis, Roche and Serono – spent about CHF 7.1 billion on researching and developing new drugs worldwide in 2001. This figure is equivalent to 17.3% of their total pharmaceutical sales.

In 2001, the three companies sold drugs worth CHF 507 million in Switzerland, just 1.2% of their global sales. Nonetheless, Novartis, Roche and Serono spent almost CHF 3.1 billion on pharmaceutical research and development in Switzerland in the same year. This represents around 43.3% of their global outlay on pharmaceutical R&D.

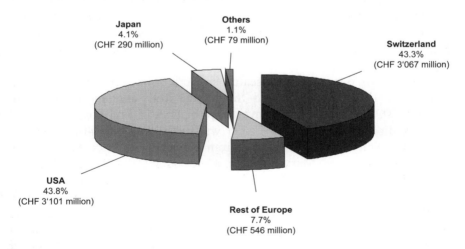

Source: Pharma Information (2002)

Fig. 41. Worldwide R&D spending by Interpharma companies in 2001.

The high outlay for research and development in Switzerland is only possible because of the high export volume in the pharmaceutical sector. In 2001, Novartis, Roche and Serono together exported around CHF 25 billion in pharmaceutical products, 90% of Switzerland's total pharmaceutical exports.

With almost CHF 3.1 billion in both Switzerland as well as the US, the three Interpharma companies invested about the same amount of capital for R&D purposes in each country. However, more recently the US and the Far East seem to have become increasingly important to the Interpharma companies, as recent R&D investments in Boston (Novartis) and Shanghai (Roche) illustrate.

Locations of Pharmaceutical R&D Abroad

As the pharmaceutical R&D pipeline is one of the key indicators for future blockbuster drugs and thus revenues, stock prices fluctuate with good or bad news emanating from the R&D pipeline. Investor pressure has led pharmaceutical companies to document their R&D activities comparatively well. Let us consider, for instance, the international R&D network of Novartis.

In early 2003, Novartis had 67 drug candidates in clinical development. About 3'000 scientists worked in 10 research centers worldwide in a number of therapeutic areas (see case study Novartis). Only 1'400 of them are employed in research centers in Switzerland, along with a comparable number in pre-clinical and clinical development (see also Zeller 2001). More than half of the R&D workforce is located outside Switzerland (see Fig. 42).

Novartis has expanded its research network with two research sites in Cambridge (Massachusetts) and Singapore. Both announcements were made in 2002. With a starting investment of US$ 250 million, the Massachusetts BioMedical Research Center will initially employ 400 scientists, some of which will be transferred from Novartis' R&D centers in New Jersey and elsewhere. Mark Fishman, a professor of medicine at Harvard Medical School, is the director of the new center. Novartis plans to expand the Cambridge site into one of the most important research campuses worldwide for the discovery of new drugs for diabetes, cardiovascular and infectious diseases. The choice to locate a new R&D site in Cambridge – as opposed to expanding the existing research center in East Hanover (New Jersey) – was made with consideration to the vast and so far untapped concentration of biomedical scientists, hospitals, research institutes,

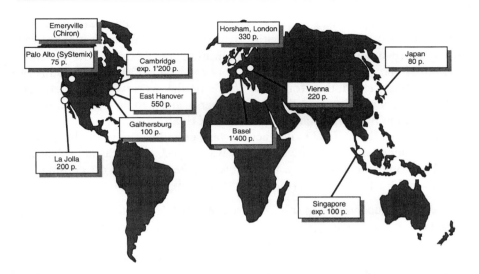

Fig. 42. The research network of Novartis in 2001.

and corporate R&D centers in Cambridge. In comparison to California, for instance, the Boston-Cambridge area also has a higher concentration of biotech firms in a five- to ten-mile radius. With the joint appointment of Mark Fishman as the new head of biomedical research at Novartis world-wide, a significant power shift has occurred from Basel to Cambridge.

The new research center for tropical diseases in Singapore followed a different rationale. Based on an agreement with the Singapore Economic Development Board (EDB), Novartis will invest a total of US$ 122 million. The research center will also receive support from EDB's US$ 600 million R&D fund, which was set up in June 2000 to promote private R&D activities in Singapore. The scientific focus is on tuberculosis and dengue fever – two illnesses particular widespread in the developing world. Historically, due to the high costs of drug discovery and development, there has been little effort in the pharmaceutical industry to fund research in this area, as financial returns were viewed as unattractive. Novartis' investment is thus also considered as a long-term commitment to improve health and prosperity in developing countries. Singapore is located on the tropical belt, and houses excellent research institutes and other corporate R&D centers. Head of Novartis Research Paul Herrling was overseeing the initial phases of the ramp-up himself, until the new director took over in Fall 2003.

Novartis is not unique in its international dispersion of R&D. To the contrary, the specific nature of high project termination risks, high development costs, and broad research needs have necessitated pharmaceutical companies to spread R&D activities over multiple locations at a comparatively early stage of R&D internationalization. Furthermore, the consolidation of the pharmaceutical industry is quite small (with the industry leader Pfizer accounting for about 7.5% of the worldwide market, see Table 4), hence internationalization has been – and will be – determined to a large extent by mergers and acquisitions of rivals.

A study of 1'021 R&D sites across various industries (including automotive, engineering, electrical, IT, software, food, chemical and pharmaceutical companies) produced the following overall results concerning international R&D locations (von Zedtwitz, Gassmann 2002):

- R&D is concentrated in the Triad regions of Europe, the United States, Japan, as well as major regional centers in South Korea, Singapore and other emerging economies along the Pacific Rim, such as China. Research is more concentrated than development. Over seventy percent (73.2%) of all research sites are located in the five regions of the Northeastern USA (New Jersey, New York, Massachusetts), California, the United Kingdom, Western Continental Europe (in particular Germany), and the Far East (Japan, South Korea). The trend of research concentration is even more apparent when only foreign research locations are considered: 87.4% operate in the Triad.
- Although the main regional centers for development largely coincide with the regional centers for research, development is more evenly distributed among European countries and the Northeastern United States, and extends into Southeast Asia, Australia, Africa, and South America. Only slightly more than half (53.4%) of all development sites are located in the eight most development-intensive countries. Development sites from 19 countries must be considered in order to account for a similar share in worldwide development (74.2%) as the top eight countries in research (73.2%).

Moreover, research and development sites of the same company are not necessarily co-located. For instance, AstraZeneca operates research as well as development units in the United States. A research unit in Waltham, Massachusetts focuses on infectious diseases. Since there is no complementary development in the US, their research findings are transferred to a development laboratory in Sweden. The 1990s have seen an effort of many large companies to consolidate their activities in order to realize synergy and coordination potential in international R&D. Transnational R&D projects are managed more easily if the R&D network consists of competence centers such as is the case for Roche or Novartis, given that complementary competencies are provided locally. With increasing complementarity of resources, competencies, and knowledge bases, as well as the division of labor and specialization of work, synergy potentials in R&D projects can be exploited.

Fig. 43 shows a subset of 193 pharmaceutical R&D laboratories of the 1'021 R&D locations studied earlier. It includes R&D locations of AHP, AstraZeneca, Boehringer Ingelheim, Eli Lilly, Eisai, Glaxo-Wellcome, Pfizer, Novartis, Novo Nordisk, Roche, Schering, and Yamanouchi. The distribution of these R&D sites shows a similar pattern to the overall set but differs in the following observations:

- In the US, R&D is focused more on the North-East and Mid-West; the relative importance of the Pacific Coast has declined;
- In Europe, R&D is more evenly distributed. Overall, Europe seems to host a greater share of development sites compared to the US;
- There are very few R&D laboratories (only 15) outside the Triad regions.

Given this data, the pharmaceutical industry is one of the most internationalized in terms of R&D locations, with one foreign R&D lab for every

Fig. 43. Locations of 193 R&D labs of 12 pharmaceutical firms (data collected from 1997-2003).

domestic lab. Pharmaceutical companies also seem to internationalize research as fast as development (albeit for different reasons). Most other industries tend to keep research at home and localize development. Although not obvious from location data alone, pharmaceutical companies also tend to organize R&D as competence-based networks, as opposed to R&D hubs (e.g., automotive and chemicals), polycentric networks (e.g., local market-dependent companies such as Royal Dutch/Shell) or centralized R&D (e.g., dominant design industries). In competence-based R&D networks, each R&D node has a clearly defined competence – and responsibility! – which it brings into the network of other R&D centers. The coordination and management of such R&D networks is more demanding and costly than rather centralized and directive R&D hubs, or the laissez-faire style of polycentric R&D networks. As a consequence, pharmaceutical companies (and many electrical and IT companies, who also favor this R&D organization) try to coordinate R&D activities across multiple levels, including the deployment of transnational project teams, platform management, informal as well as formal network techniques, etc. The next chapters illustrate some typical problems in international R&D and related management techniques.

Three Principal Problems of International R&D

When people and teams are geographically apart, problems of coordination and communication become more important. In international R&D, some of the most significant problems are:

1. Lack of face-to-face time
2. Cultural differences
3. Lack of trust

Lack of face-to-face time

People are more creative when they can interact with colleagues with whom they can trust, bounce ideas off, and explain themselves in a variety of ways. In dispersed teams, access and contact to colleagues is restricted, communication is often asynchronous and limited to information and communication technologies, such as the telephone. This is a major problem particularly in the early phases of R&D, when formal creativity techniques such as brainstorming or informal ones such as water cooler discussions are key ingredients to finding effective solutions. Information and communication technologies are also good for the exchange of explicit, data-driven information only, but fail at providing communication that is rich in experience in multiple communication dimensions, such as interactive shared-access graphics, three-dimensionality, haptic and sensory information, etc.

Lack of face time can already inhibit R&D work in non-international settings. For instance, after a large pharmaceutical company redesigned one of their R&D centers, management decided it would be a good idea to allow their scientists to work longer in their labs, ordering the cafeterias on each lab floor to provide lunch-bags for anyone who wished. As a positive side effect, the cafeterias could be made smaller as it had to accommodate fewer people. Consequently, scientists picked up their lunches, retreated to their benches and missed out on the opportunity to share their insights informally over lunch. When this became apparent, management abolished the lunch-bag option. Additionally, they closed most lab floor cafeterias and opened a large central cafeteria on a single floor. Scientists now meet colleagues and peers from different departments and labs, improving informal exchange of knowledge and information.

Cultural differences

It is all too obvious that we are different, and regional commonalities of these differences are often denoted by culture. There are two important notions for international R&D work in culture:

1. Cultural differences making cooperation more difficult.
2. Different cultures and their relation to innovation and creativity.

The first source of problems has been described by Hofstede (1980) in his work on cultural distances between countries. Surveying 88'000 IBM employees, he arrived at five cultural dimensions that explained different behavioral preferences (see Fig. 44). Although some of us may share the same perception of, for example, the importance of hierarchy and ranks, we may have a very different opinion when it comes to values on individualism or collectivism. Thus we all differ from each other, but in different ways. This makes managing multi-cultural teams not particularly easy.

The second source of problems has been research by Shane (1992 and 1993), who studied the rate of invention by people from 33 different nations. He found that people from individualistic and non-hierarchical societies are more inventive (measured in patents per capita) than other societies. By implication, some societies may have a cultural comparative advantage in inventiveness, and corporations should consider establishing

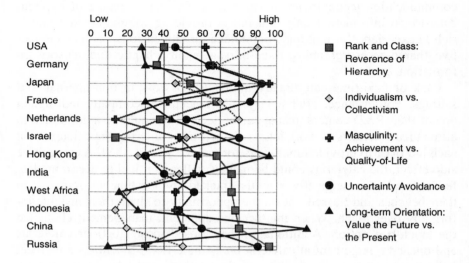

Fig. 44. Cultural differences among countries (adapted from Hofstede 1980).

R&D centers in these countries. Also, it means that companies may not be able to increase the rates of innovation simply by increasing the amount of money spent on R&D in a given country. Shane also found that per capita income was more important than industrial structure in determining national rates of innovation, indicating that as nations become wealthier, they also become more innovative. Shane's findings certainly have strong implications for the selection of individuals in certain phases of R&D and innovation work, as well as consideration of the R&D mission when choosing a location for a new R&D site.

Lack of trust

Trust is a vital ingredient in R&D work where intellectual property is often not yet claimed or clearly assigned. Lack of trust leads to secrecy, keeping potentially good ideas to oneself, and consequently to unexploited opportunities of innovation. There are many ways to build trust in teams, but separating individual team members is certainly not one of them. Through physical distance, individuals cannot communicate as often and as well as they used to, they do not share common work space or referential frameworks, and they may become absorbed more in the local R&D setting rather than as feeling part of the international R&D project. Lack of trust is a great barrier to innovation.

How can transnational R&D teams counteract the loss of trust? First of all, it is difficult enough to establish trust in any team. This is, however, a precondition for any high-performing team. The four stages of group development start with 'forming', followed by 'storming', 'norming', and eventually 'performing' (see e.g., West 1998). The 'forming' stage is critically dependent on good communication, informal get-togethers, and creating a unique project spirit. This is difficult to achieve at a distance for truly innovative projects, and only possible in distance teams if scientific or technical domains provide a common bracket and work interdependencies are minimal (see e.g., Gassmann, von Zedtwitz 2003).

Thus, even the most transnational R&D team will have to resort to travel, at least for some of its members. Typically, a kick-off meeting, which should last at least a day and better if it allows social time for a dinner, starts the actual project work. Trust can be built here, or at least a working relationship can be established. Once the team disperses again, communication will be limited to information and communication technologies, which are good for exchanging explicit information but inappropriate for establishing a tacit communication dimension. Thus, trust is likely to diminish, and a new meeting must take place (e.g., a milestone meeting or review) to allow time for building mutual respect and confidence (see Fig. 45 for a simplified representation of this scheme).

How much time that should be allowed to pass is unclear. De Meyer (1991) coined the term 'half-time of trust' to denote the period of time in

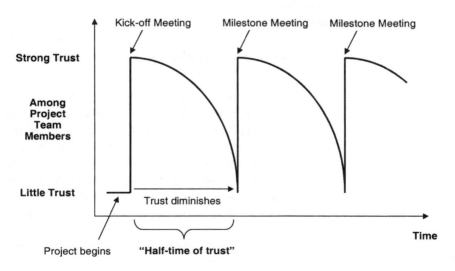

Fig. 45. Halt-time of trust: E-mail is not enough in coordinating a high-performance team.

which trust is halved. R&D managers in the engineering and automotive industries indicated that two to three full-team meetings per year are appropriate to maintain a common team spirit. This must be supported by more frequent visits to each subteam by the overall team manager or project integrator. Other, more subtle means of building common team brackets, such as a company-wide recognition like a 'Golden Badge' or 'High Risk' team, may sustain team identity, and certainly involves the support of top management.

Conclusions

Outsourcing in pharmaceutical R&D is extremely complex. In addition, managing the outsourcing partner can be very cumbersome depending on the field of collaboration. Thus, many companies still use outsourcing only to manage peak resource shortages despite its potential to help improve the overall R&D performance.

R&D organizations have developed from centralized and geographically confined towards distributed and open structures. Some of the most frequent challenges that arise during R&D internationalization cover the following six fundamental dilemmas:

- Local versus global;
- Process versus hierarchy;
- Creativity versus discipline;
- Control versus open source;
- Face to face versus information and communication technologies;
- Short-term versus long-term.

Dilemmas are not negative per se. To the contrary, in a dilemma both alternative courses of action are equally valuable. The various approaches to managing these dilemmas – including those that attempt to eliminate them altogether – have given rise to an impressive body of know-how among R&D managers and R&D scientists. However, one constant can be stated: Looking ten years ahead, regardless of the rapid evolution of modern technologies, new organizational concepts and even more efficient tools, the individual and teams will remain at the core of international management of innovation.

The key lessons learned for managing global R&D in the pharmaceutical industry can be classified as follows:

- Localization of management resources;

- Flat and flexible organizations;
- Introduction of local culture of innovation and know-how;
- Challenging projects coupled with bottom-up creativity;
- Personal interactions more important in decentralized R&D;
- Synchronization of international drug development by means of transnational project management in order to shorten R&D cycles;
- Worldwide integrated R&D data management;
- Acquisition of external ideas and projects as important as internal R&D;
- International teams require new organizations;
- Manage platforms, not individual R&D projects;
- Foster networking and collaboration.

In conclusion, the pharmaceutical industry is one of the most advanced in terms of R&D internationalization, and one of the most specific when it comes to regulation and significance of science and technology. R&D management is a key ingredient to success, and the high stakes of the drug approval and medical safety have made the pharmaceutical innovation pipeline one of the best understood R&D engines. However, there is still untapped potential to improve this engine with new technologies, new managerial approaches, and new scientific talent drawn from countries around the world.

VI. Management Answers to Pharmaceutical R&D Challenges

„PhRMA member companies are expected to invest more than US$ 30 billion to discover and develop new medicines. These numbers give weight to the real but intangible quality that defines our industry: hope. "

Alan F. Holmer,
President of Pharmaceutical Research and Manufacturers of America (PhRMA), 1998

Managing the Research-to-Development Handover

Time-to-market is extremely important in breakthrough pharmaceuticals: the first in the market captures 40-60% of the market, and the second only around 15%. Coming in behind third means a negative business.

Roche therefore puts great emphasis on development speed. "Projects first, budgets second", said Roche's former Head of R&D Controlling, Alfons Wunschheim. Delaying market introduction of a blockbuster medicine by two months not only involves the risk that a competitor seizes significant market share, it also means a net loss of US$ 100 million, or almost US$ 2 million a day.

In research, integrated disease units (IDUs) have been formed which have all the necessary functions and technologies to bring projects to a state where they can be handed over to development. The IDUs have a great deal of autonomy over how they achieve the goals that are set by the Research Board. Development candidates must be active, efficient, and safe. These requirements have been tested in animals.

The Research Board selects prospective development candidates and proposes them to the Product Development Board. Critical parameters are human compatibility, a medical need, and a business case. Not all projects can be proposed, and some projects are returned to research for later con-

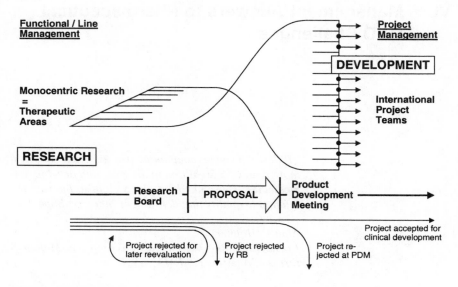

Source: von Zedtwitz (1999)

Fig. 46. Project handover between research and development at Roche.

sideration or rework. The earlier a no-go decision can be taken the better, since extending ill-fated research projects only wastes money (Fig. 46).

The Product Development Board evaluates the development candidates proposed by the Research Board. Some of the candidates are accepted, others are turned away. Until recently, these diverted candidates have been divested. It is currently under discussion whether Roche should sell them to competing pharmaceutical companies. Accepted development candidates, however, enter the International Drug Development System (IDDS) which guides them through the various clinical and regulatory development stages.

Each development project team is responsible for developing their own budget, since it is the individual members of the team who know best about the costs of their project (project driven budgeting). The project development board adjusts the project budget for the overall development portfolio. The development activities are adjusted to the financial frame set by the available budget. The resource allocation by the board is a revolving activity. It must be decided several times per year for each project whether to continue a project and with what intensity.

For each development project a Drug Development Plan is set up, describing and defining all activities needed to reach the next decision point.

The sum of the costs of anticipated resources, support activities, and indirect costs is the estimated total costs of the project for the given budget period. This sum is calculated under the assumption that all milestones will be successfully reached, and therefore exceeds the overall development budget. But since attrition is still very high in development, most projects will be eliminated at one of the many decision points during the budget period.

The probability of passing a given decision point can be estimated from past experience and is dependent on the project phase. 'Factoring' is the application of the probability percentage to the resources and costs for the time after the decision point. The full budget costs before the decision points and the factored costs after the decision point will provide the budget costs for the project in the given project period. The sum of all factored project costs will provide the necessary budget and must be compared to the budget framework. Exceeding the budget framework will result in revision of the portfolio and possibly in the termination of entire development projects.

The high attrition rate demands that R&D resources are well spent and unsuccessful projects terminated quickly. A predefined and elaborate R&D process has been developed, and every deviation from the expected results during the testing is to be detected and investigated. If a drug candidate fails during the development phase it is withdrawn entirely from further testing. Unlike in the automobile industry, drugs are not modular products where a faulty stick shift can be replaced without throwing the entire car design away. In pharmaceutical R&D, drug design cannot be changed. This necessitates high up-front investment for each drug candidate.

Managing Human Resources

> *„One way we try to foster innovation – both the technological innovation and the organizational innovation – is to align our business objectives with our ideals. People do a better job when they believe in what they do – not just enriching shareholders. "*
>
> *Daniel Vasella,*
> *CEO of Novartis, 2002*

Strategic pipeline management requires a strategic approach to managing researchers and research managers. Given the knowledge-intensive nature of pharmaceutical R&D, the management of human resources in pharmaceuticals has traditionally focused on developing specialists and reducing the (unwanted) flow of information beyond predetermined boundaries. More recently, however, the role of human resources has become to include, among others, personnel assessment and training, knowledge management, and strategic leadership development. All of these necessitate a more open-minded approach to managing people.

In the past decades, a paradigm shift has occurred in science. With the end of the cold war, fundamental industrial research ran out of government funds. At the same time, new entrepreneurial opportunities in the New Economy meant that young researchers started to commercialize their technologies themselves. Science became more open partly because of necessity (research labs reaching out for collaboration partners to sustain their innovation funnels) or because of opportunity (graduate students turned entrepreneurs seeking complementary technologies to start new businesses). While the pharmaceutical industry has followed or even developed this trend in outsourcing some of their basic research to biotechnology companies, they have often failed to rethink their internal R&D organizations to reflect the new times.

Small, multi-disciplinary teams have been at the core of the success of biotechnology start-ups or the introduction of new technologies. Large research and development departments are often good at administrating long-term research efforts, but incapable of flexible decision-making and absorption and dissemination of innovative ideas. Job rotation and training programs educate the individual researcher about other activities in the company, and allow him or her to make better and faster decisions: i.e., making decisions where the action is. For example, Bayer is known for their job rotation practice, where every researcher is only allowed to stay for a maximum of 5 years in the same position. Japanese pharmaceutical companies are also applying sophisticated job rotation programs. However, in many pharmaceutical companies, most of the researchers only have contact with the HR department once in a lifetime: at the moment they are hired.

Fostering creativity is another important aspect in managing human resources. Scientists spend only an estimated 11% of their time on research, and only 2% on new research. Chemists, microbiologists, medical doctors, and marketing experts should collaborate in new projects to learn from each other about the nature of their businesses. It is a long-established fact that interdisciplinary teams are better at innovation. Furthermore, it has been shown that creativity in pharmaceutical R&D is more likely in smaller research teams. The trend towards mega-mergers and ever larger companies forces pharmaceutical R&D management to bear in mind this parameter of creativeness.

Every employee in R&D should ask himself what his or her contribution could be across all levels of the R&D process. This approach may require abandoning the structured linear process and move towards more group- and team-oriented R&D work. Feedback loops (i.e., from the clinical trials back to basic research and the screening stages) have to be established. Post-project reviews identify not only technical but also managerial areas of improvement. The overall goal of R&D should not be to be innovative but to generate products which are successful on the market.

In addition, HR has an obligation to develop future project managers and business leaders. HR should act as a consultant to department heads and group managers how to best develop and promote talented subordinates. Exit interviews still focus too much on the past and too little on improvements for future positions and future successors. Where HR faces resistance from conservative functional managers, they should insist on the greater picture of developing motivated and educated individuals rather than stagnating technical functionaries (who are likely to leave the company for a competitor who may offer a better career path). Strategic HR management in pharmaceuticals addresses these issues upfront, and develops a career roadmap for talented individuals who can grow through R&D projects, business development, as well as marketing and sales experience, in order to become the future R&D leaders that pharmaceutical companies need ten to fifteen years from now.

Managing Projects and the Portfolio

The principal task of portfolio management is to ensure that a well-balanced combination of projects makes use of the company's competencies and is directed at defined therapeutic areas and profitable markets. Access to networks in clinics and market opinion is a key success factor during this activity.

Once an overall R&D strategy has been defined, the first step in pharmaceutical project management is to select and evaluate the right projects. Many companies rely on the net-present-value method in order to select projects. This method projects future cash in-flows and out-flows and discounts the balance of each year's net cash-flow to the present date by the relative costs thereby incurred.

BASF Pharma (the pharmaceutical division of BASF later acquired by Abbott in March 2001) established the following methodology to evaluate projects. In order to traceably project revenues, a target-product profile has to be established first in collaboration with research, development and marketing departments. A target-profile is determined by the therapeutical area, impact-profile, scientific data for the registration authorities, competitive landscape, as well as the medical requirements and market expectations. Based upon the target-profile, a development plan can be derived including the necessary time-schedules, milestones, resources and activities, as well as – based on the marketing plan – the respective revenue expectations. This allows the connection of qualitative factors (such as market attractiveness or competitive position) with quantitative factors (such as clinical data, market potential, market share, price expectations) in order to create cost-revenue plans and, hence, to set-up a free-cash-flow plan for each particular project. Simultaneously, a discussion and critical analysis of the departments that participate during the development (such as clinical development, marketing, production, authorization) is launched. The interdisciplinary appraisal of all available data and facts is the foremost reason for this step. The purpose of valuation is ultimately to gain an understanding and not to arrive at a number.

In order to generate the required data, only projects from the development stage 'clinical phase 2' onward will be included into the evaluation. At this point in time, the data available can describe and characterize the project in its respective market. This could include questions of the pharmacological impact-profile, which allow a firm to derive the therapeutic indication as well as assumptions about the daily dosages, which allow to predict detailed projections about prices and production. Fig. 47 illustrates this type of revenue planning tool.

The costs of production (without depreciation) are determined by using standard data, which are based upon average daily dosages according to clinical studies. The planning of the marketing costs is done simultaneously, which can be derived from the respective marketing-mix. In case additional investments in property plant and equipment are necessary or a significant impact on the working capital can be expected (e.g., long payment horizons in the hospital business, in some European countries more than 1 or 2 years), they will have to be considered as 'cash out'. The calculated annual free-cash-flow is discounted by using the weighted-average cost of capital model. The planning horizon is about 10 to 15 years.

Novartis evaluates projects by comparing the potential value and expected performance of the projects. The potential value includes considerations about the market, competitiveness and/or feasibility. Performance parameters relate to the capabilities of the team, overall project objectives and the patent position among others. This approach is applicable as well to technology platforms.

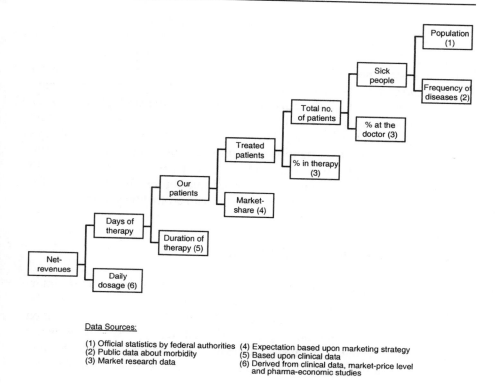

Data Sources:

(1) Official statistics by federal authorities   (4) Expectation based upon marketing strategy
(2) Public data about morbidity   (5) Based upon clinical data
(3) Market research data   (6) Derived from clinical data, market-price level
   and pharma-economic studies

Source: Völker (2001)

Fig. 47. Determination of expected product revenues at BASF Pharma.

In some cases, R&D projects offer options that go beyond the actual project. For example, the development of a new product could be tied to the development of a new process, which has a certain probability to be used for the development of other products in the future. In situations like these, option-values have to be added to the direct value of a particular project. In recent years, the real options approach has frequently been discussed in valuing pharmaceutical R&D projects. However, it has not yet found broad acceptance.

Portfolio management in pharmaceutical R&D requires a combination of risk-taking and risk-hedging. A full and solid pipeline of prospective products is the goal of every pharmaceutical company, and it is generally believed that the more new chemical entities pass through the pipeline and eventually enter the market, the better. However, the risk of market failure is increasing as most companies are targeting the same product areas and launching their products at closer intervals to each other. Markets are quickly crowded with competing products. For instance, four new angiotensin products (Diovan, Teveten, Aprovel, and Atacand) were recently introduced in a period of months. Therefore, a profound portfolio management system not only requires a focus on the number of new chemical entities, but also an adjustment in the way in which medicines are profiled and marketed. For example, Pfizer does not pursue the strategy of a leader in the number of market introductions but tries to maximize the commercial success of each new molecular entity. Hence, successful firms always allocate their resources, oftentimes via in-licensing agreements, to a limited number of high-value and innovative drugs which are expected to have significant sales potential. As pointed out before, the Holy Grail for any pharmaceutical company is to come up with a blockbuster product.

Managing Outsourcing Activities

Outsourcing requires the establishment of an effective and efficient interface between the pharmaceutical company and the service provider. For synthesis services, it has been shown that the chemical structure (as written on paper) represents the most appropriate interface. The service provider takes over the synthetic chemistry of the development process and delivers the chemical substances back to the pharmaceutical company (Fig. 48).

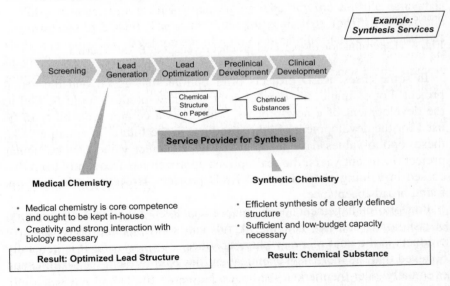

Fig. 48. Interface between pharmaceutical company and pharmaceutical service provider: Example of synthesis services provided by Solvias.

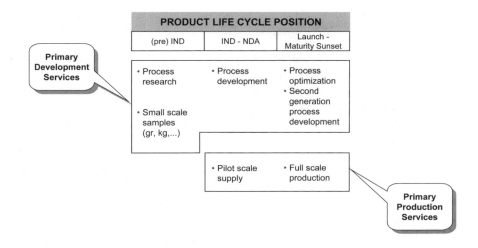

Fig. 49. Distinction between development and production services at Solvias.

However, a clear distinction must be drawn between development services and production services in outsourcing drug development activities. Primary development services include process research & development, development of second generation processes as well as the supply of pre-clinical trial quantities. Primary production related services are dealing with the full scale supply of intermediates and active pharmaceutical ingredients (APIs) at various stages of the product lifecycle (Fig. 49).

Major concerns of pharmaceutical companies, which in turn should be addressed by the pharmaceutical service provider, include complexity and efficiency, intellectual property and royalties, exclusivity and costs. Hence, the success factors for service providers imply a clear definition of efficient and highly standardized processes and contracts. Furthermore, a co-operation agreement has to be signed which avoids royalties and leaves all intellectual property at the pharmaceutical company. Clear non-disclosure agreements and non-competitive agreements in the field of chemical substances have to be established; as well as a comprehensive and full cost transparency.

In reality, three different cooperation models exist between the pharmaceutical company and the pharmaceutical service provider, depending on the amount and price of services provided (Fig. 50). With the preferred partnership model, the customer (pharmaceutical company) enters into preferential agreements with a handful of selected, strategic suppliers acting almost as 'facility managers'. However, this model might clash with the pharmaceutical company's desire to keep a certain level of freedom, as

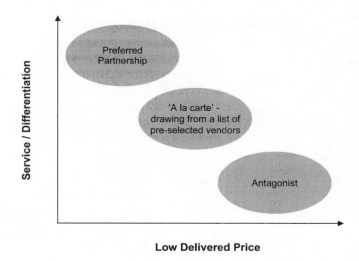

Low Delivered Price

Fig. 50. Main models of customer-vendor interaction in outsourcing pharmaceutical R&D (Example: Solvias).

well as to maintain a healthy bargaining power vis-à-vis vendors. The second model, the 'a la carte'- drawing from a list of pre-selected vendors, is usually applied if no single supplier is able to provide the breadth of capabilities required by the pharmaceutical company to serve its full spectrum of needs. Overdependence on a single vendor should be avoided so as to spread risks and maintain a healthy leverage. The best vendor for each area of activity should be retained by the customer. The antagonist-model provides the pharmaceutical company with the advantage that the vendors (service providers) are systematically put into competition and, hence, the best price for the offered service can be secured.

No matter which model and what degree of outsourcing is being applied, the service provider should always be fully integrated into the processes and structures of the pharmaceutical company. Areas with a high potential of standardization are of interest for outsourcing, such as processes, interfaces, contracts, and incentives. If, however, there is a high level of complexity in the processes between service provider and pharmaceutical company, or if there are interfaces which are difficult to define, the tendency towards outsourcing declines. In the future, it is expected that external service providers will temporarily be integrated into internal R&D teams and, hence, will be able to provide more flexibly and timely support for R&D projects. The responsibility for the effective and efficient coordination of all internal and external resources as well as the know-how and expertise transfer will be represented by internal project management, which is regarded as a core competence by pharmaceutical companies.

There are different consequences of this paradigm shift. Barriers between the individual organization units and the various companies will disappear. In the long run, pharmaceutical and biotechnology companies will have a greater possibility to buy standardized and established external services or new and innovative methods around chemical synthesis along the entire value chain in pharmaceutical R&D. Therefore, pharmaceutical R&D will become leaner and avoid the building and maintaining of research infrastructure which is used in parallel.

Solvias: Spin-off as Outsourcing Partner

Solvias was created through the spin-off of a scientific competence center of Novartis in October 1999 and is a totally independent company owned by the Solvias management. The company employs around 250 highly qualified employees.

Solvias offers services to the pharmaceutical industry mainly in the areas of research and development, production and quality control. The company's services include a variety of chemical, physical and biological services – from synthesis to analytics.

Solvias provides its services to companies from the pharmaceutical, agricultural, chemical and food industries as well as government authorities and institutes. Clients include Beiersdorf, Boehringer Ingelheim, Roche, Shell and Wella among others.

Managing Intellectual Property Rights

The 40 leading pharmaceutical firms worldwide have been granted on average 5.8 patents per thousand employees. In 2001, the US accounted for approximately 45% of all pharmaceutical patents that were issued. Japan and Germany both contributed around 10% of patents, followed by the UK with 7% and France with 5%. Looking at company trends, US companies continue to dominate patent approvals in the US. The proportion of US pharmaceutical patents issued to US and Japanese companies has increased over the last 20 years, while the proportion issued to European companies has declined: Between 1980 and 1984, US companies were issued around

50% of patents, Japanese companies 13% and EU companies 29%. However, between 1990 and 1994, the proportion of patents issued to US and Japanese companies increased to 55% and 15% respectively, while the proportion issued to EU companies fell to 24% (Reuters 2002).

Leading therapy areas for patent approval worldwide were infectious disease (15%), oncology (14%), cardiovascular disease (10%), neurology (10%), and immune disorders (8%). The distribution of patents across therapy areas largely reflects the balance of the pipeline, and is closely matched to relative unmet need and market opportunity (Reuters 2002).

Besides making inventions available to the public, patents also protect innovators against imitation and replication of their innovations and knowledge. Pharmaceutical products can easily be copied or imitated because it is not difficult to analyze a pharmaceutical product and its respective substances. Due to the significant R&D spending in the pharmaceutical industry and the high risks associated with new drug development, patent protection and the subsequent management of intellectual property is particularly important for this industry. As mentioned earlier, studies have shown that patents are the most effective means of appropriation and found that 65% of pharmaceutical inventions would not have been introduced without patent protection, compared to a cross-industry average of 8% (Reuters 2002).

International patent legislation typically encompasses four statutory classes of patentable inventions that are relevant to the pharmaceutical industry (see Reuters 2003b):

- Process patents;
- Product patents;
- Composition patents;
- Use patents.

Process claims refer to the method used to produce a pharmaceutical product rather than to the chemical itself. As it may be possible to develop the same chemical through several different methods, it is often difficult to protect pharmaceutical products solely with process patents or to prove infringement of process patents. Product patents refer to tangible products. Generally, these are commercially viable entities that are ready to be launched or already on the market.

In the pharmaceutical industry, patents are usually applied to medical devices, such as drug delivery mechanisms, since few manufacturers would want to wait until they perform clinical trials on a compound to apply for patent protection.

In Switzerland, three different types of innovations can be patented (Leutenegger 1994):

1. Chemical processes for the production of substances;
2. New chemical substances and medicaments with new chemical substances;
3. Supplements with known chemical substances without a pharmaceutical scope.

New substances or new processes receive patent protection for a period of 20 years. However, considering the average time for a new drug development in the pharmaceutical industry is up to 13 years, the major problem regarding patent protection becomes obvious: the timing of the patent. If a company files for a patent too early, the period when it can market and sell the drug exclusively will automatically be reduced. This is particularly important in light of the fact that pharmaceutical companies only have a relatively short time to market their products and generate a return on their high initial investments. On the other hand, if a company files too late for a patent, it risks losing the invention to competitors. In practice, this means that the effective period of patent protection is rarely more than 8 years in the pharmaceutical industry (see also page 76).

Patent protection is particularly important in the area of biotechnology. Several ethical questions arise that are not yet covered by existing patent laws and/or acts, including the ownership of genes and whether genes can be patented at all. However, the Swiss Ethics Committee on Non-Human Gene Technology recently came to the conclusion that intellectual achievements in the area of biotechnology are allowed to be protected. This is justified by the overall purpose of the patent act to support research in the best interest of the public.

Due to the fact that Switzerland recently has experienced a biotech-boom and has a real chance to be among the leading nations worldwide in the biotechnology sector, the coming revision of the current patent act is overdue. The Swiss patent act should be adapted to the EU-guideline regarding the security of biotechnological inventions. While the revision will not broaden the patentability, it will broaden the focus of the patent act to include all aspects dealing with the life of humans, animals and plants.

According to Interpharma secretary general Thomas Cueni, it is, hence, just an affirmation of today's practice. Moreover, it is already possible today to receive patents for biotechnological inventions, such as a gene, a genetically changed plant, a biotechnological process or a microorganism. The new Swiss patent revision clarifies some open questions regarding the interpretation of already existing clauses. However, the revision will also cover what will be excluded from patenting: processes regarding cloning of human beings, processes regarding changes of the genetic identity of human beings, as well as the usage of human embryos for industrial or commercial purposes.

Intellectual Property Management at Bayer

Bayer posted revenues of about €30 billion in 2002 (pharmaceuticals accounted for €3.7 billion) and employs 120'000 people worldwide. The entire group spent around €2.5 billion on R&D.

Bayer looks at intellectual property as a product of its own. Every intellectual property thus needs its own marketing plan. The intellectual property products are typically spin-offs, 'white-space' developments or technologies (i.e., devices or methods) that are no longer being used by Bayer's business units. When selling the products, Bayer strictly follows the rule, 'don't try to sell any leftovers'.

Bayer developed a four-stage process to decide if certain know-how or a certain technology can be utilized externally. First, Bayer asks if the respective know-how/technology is a surplus product. If yes, the second stage contemplates if the know-how is strategically valuable for any core activity of Bayer's business units. If it is not, the third stage analyzes if the respective technology could be easily brought to a potentially attractive market. If this stage is answered with a yes, the final stage observes if the know-how is not strategically valuable for any other business unit at Bayer. If the intellectual property passes all four stages, it can be marketed outside of Bayer, otherwise it is retained in-house.

Regarding the valuation of the intellectual property, Bayer differentiates between business licenses, product licenses, and technology licenses. The value of business and product licenses, which deal with entire businesses and/or products, can easily be determined by using the scenario technique. The value of technology licenses, however, is much more complicated to estimate and done by looking at the technology maturity and the commercial risk. The combination of both allows for a fairly good estimate. Finally, the marketing plan includes the intellectual property utilization strategy, which could include cross-licensing agreements, royalty payments, cash payments, or equity offerings.

Managing R&D Strategy at Schering

All key features of Schering's present R&D management were established between 1990 and 1994. These features were established to respond to the business requirements of fast, synchronized global drug development and market entry, to the harmonization of international regulatory requirements, and to rescue limitations in R&D, which are a consequence of cost increases due to increased regulatory requirements (Müller (2000) of Project Coordination at Schering).

Rather than a clear-cut centralized organization with direct power over all R&D facilities, a decentralized organization coordinated by corporate management processes and a strong International Project Management was chosen. This method was chosen to best combine global R&D capabilities and flexible responses to meet local needs.

Strategic R&D management is looked after at board level in the Portfolio Board and includes setting of R&D strategy, decisions on major R&D cooperations, decisions on initiation and start of phase III of development projects, and yearly prioritization as well as continuous adjustments of prioritization for the whole portfolio of development projects (Fig. 51). Portfolio Board decisions concerning research are operationalized by the International Research Management Conference (chaired by the Executive

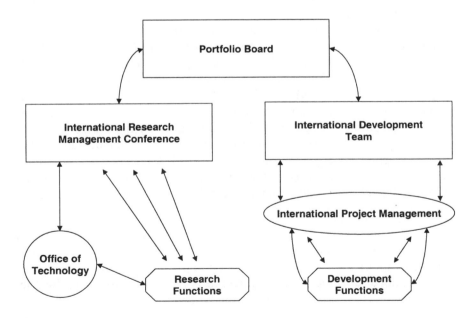

Fig. 51. Coordination of pharmaceutical R&D management at Schering.

Board Member of R&D), which takes care of research budget setting and control, all decisions concerning research projects and research cooperations (below Portfolio Board-level), and periodical project reviews.

Portfolio Board-decisions concerning development projects are operationalized by the International Development Team, chaired by the head of International Project Management and represent all major resource-holders in international R&D. The International Development Team closely interacts with International Project Management and its responsibilities cover development budget planning and control, all operational decisions concerning development projects, and all operational issues concerning the international R&D organization and management processes in R&D. The International Development Team also monitors the composition and performance of the International Project Teams.

Disciplinary and functional reporting lines are dissociated in many parts of the R&D organization. While all headquarters' R&D function report directly to the Executive Board Member of R&D, functions located in the affiliates discipline report to the local hierarchy. Functional reporting, however, in the case of research, is a task for the Executive Board Member of R&D and, in the case of development, for the International Development Team.

Core members of the International Project Teams disciplinary report to their home-based and functionally report to their respective international project manager.

Proposals concerning new R&D projects can come from all parts of the organization. They are, however, in the case of research projects, subject to formal proposal-agreement processes, organized by the International Research Management Conference, or, in the case of development projects, subject to the formats and processes established by International Project Management. Decisions on new development projects are recommended by the International Development Team and made by the Portfolio Board. Local projects are possible, but no R&D project may be conducted without a decision from either the International Research Management Conference (research) or the International Development Team/Portfolio Board (development), and all milestone decisions are subject to the respective corporate processes.

1. International research coordination below the level of the International Research Management Conference (i.e., on project/program level) is done by international research project groups.
2. International development coordination is the responsibility of International Project Management, supported by coordinators in the affiliates.

Worldwide networking with academic and commercial R&D institutes and, search activities for project and product opportunities, are supported strategically and have become progressively important and complex. Therefore, an Office of Technology (a total of 15 employees, based in Berlin, USA and Japan) was established, which conducts all scientific intelligence, networking and search activities on behalf of the Strategic Business Units and of the R&D functions. The Office of Technology defines areas of interest with its partners in the R&D organization, and within these areas of interest proactively provides the R&D organization with scientific intelligence and cooperation opportunities. An international management process has been established, along which the Office of Technology interfaces with the R&D organization, with Corporate Licensing and the decision-making bodies. After identification of concrete cooperation opportunities, the Office of Technology runs the initial negotiations and, after the contracts have been signed, provides also contract management services.

Managing Virtual Project Management Pools at Roche

The systematic promotion of human resource development strategies can be backed up by a specialized project management department (Fig. 52). Hoffmann-La Roche's Pharma Division established a department called 'International Project Management' which coordinates a resource pool of about 50 project managers for all R&D projects worldwide. This department consumes about 30% of the pharmaceutical R&D expenditures and has high strategic importance to the innovative potential of this business.

Every project manager is assigned to this geographically decentralized department. The director of this 'virtual' resource pool assigns their people as managers to projects as part of a global program to ensure standards in quality and project procedures. Upon completion of the project, a project manager is returned to the resource pool. As there are more projects in the pipeline than managers available, they are immediately reassigned to a new project.

Since this new department reports directly to the board, the internal position of R&D project managers is improved. The original director of the 'International Project Management Department' was the wife of the then R&D director at board level. The establishment of a project manager pool is a clear signal for empowering one of the scarcest competitive resources. Roche manages to retain much of the valuable procedural know-how of how to conduct and lead international projects. Not only is this done on a

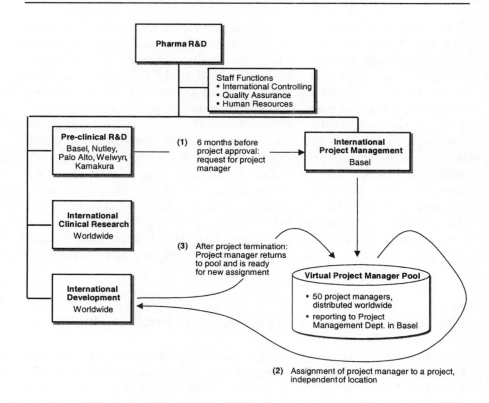

Fig. 52. Project management department as a virtual project management pool.

project level, but is also placed in a position where it can be reapplied when needed. Project offices are especially valuable when projects are very long, sometimes up to 15 years as in the pharmaceutical industry. No individual is able to carry out more than 2 or 3 projects. In a project office one can learn from dozens of projects.

The director of the 'International Project Management Department' is also a member of the International Project Committee, which decides over the roughly 60 global R&D projects at Roche Pharma. The director assumes a role as interpreter or liaison between project managers and top management, thus representing the interests of international project management at Roche. This virtual pool promotes the project management idea: experienced project managers are dispersed around the world and move from project to project – no matter where the project will be conducted.

Managing Uncertainty at Roche

Pharmaceutical research is moving away from the classical concept of having expertise in a certain disease area towards increasingly applied research. New expert knowledge and basic research are being brought into research organizations by collaborations and interactions with universities and small biotechnology companies. In addition, more emphasis is put on providing novel tools for research such as high-throughput screening, genomics and combinatorial chemistry. Especially at the front-end of R&D, virtual partnerships are entered with biotechnology companies.

The goals of virtual R&D partnership are a higher flexibility to choose the best R&D service providers, spreading of risk and costs, and economies of scale and scope. Companies try to reduce their fixed costs through transfer of less intensively utilized services to learning partner companies. This has two major advantages, namely

1. A reduction of internal complexity due to concentration, and
2. A reduction of external interfaces, since the task is now shared with the partner companies.

Roche outsourced much of the R&D process to specialized partners and suppliers, or has set-up focused R&D service providers. Examples of spin-offs of corporate R&D at Roche include Actelion and BioXell. In 1996, Roche established Protodigm, a 'virtual drug development company' (Hofmann 1997) in London. In one instance, Protodigm learned of a certain molecule, a prospective new medical substance, discovered in a university laboratory and then facilitated further research by guiding the R&D process. It contacted specialized companies to test the substance, coordinated the first clinical trials, and contracted out production, second-stage clinical development, manufacturability tests, drug registration, marketing, and even sales.

The ten Protodigm employees simultaneously oversaw three future drugs in various stages of pharmaceutical development. Since Protodigm chose the most qualified subcontractor for each stage of R&D, Roche expected a reduction in R&D costs and development time. The objective was to cut R&D costs by 40% without jeopardizing the already tight development schedule. Protodigm became Fulcrum-Pharma in 2001, expanding to offices in Japan and the US. Roche was not the only pharmaceutical company experimenting with virtual R&D: Merck was said to have saved US$ 170 million with this type of outsourcing in 1996 alone.

Behind this tendency is a fundamental change in the pharmaceutical industry: Basic research and coordination of clinical trials is increasingly being sourced out to universities or specialized companies. The industry is changing from vertically integrated competition towards more horizontal-type competition like the PC industry. Sophisticated physical models replace trial and error experiments through simulation on powerful computers.

Virtual R&D is facilitated by a shared information and communication technologies network (to expedite information and data exchange), the standardization of interfaces, and the high quality of the work carried out by the different members of the network (Jaikumar, Upton 1993). Information in the form of knowledge about technologies and products, customer feedback, product tests, research results, and markets, all must be collected, analyzed, and transferred. This information must be available in a codified, quantified or explicit form (see Nonaka, Takeuchi 1995). Implicit or tacit knowledge, which is difficult to articulate because of its ambiguity and context-relatedness, is much harder to transfer. Systemic innovation with its late 'freezing points' requires the interaction and integration of different knowledge sources and presents a great challenge for multi-site R&D.

Therefore, R&D can be 'virtualized' only if innovation is autonomous, if there are few interdependencies between parallel work tasks. Systemic innovations (i.e., R&D that involves the realization and adaptation of complementing technologies with complex interfaces) are more effectively done in large companies with central R&D. If an autonomous innovation is carried out by a centralized organization, the company is usually outrun by small firms or large decentralized companies.

Virtual R&D has thus grown in importance, in particular in industries characterized by rapidly advancing technologies, relative scarcity of technical talent, and the presence of more and more codified information in the innovation process: mostly in the electronics, information technology, software, pharmaceutical and chemical industries.

Managing Know-how Transfer at Kao

We illustrate the management of know-how transfer with an example of how the Japanese chemical company Kao conducted an 18-month-development project of hair cosmetics treatment. While such projects had predominantly been carried out in Japan, local adaptation for culture, different treatment styles, and physiological differences required the integration of R&D in local markets. Concept development and advanced research still took place in Tokyo, but much of the actual product develop-

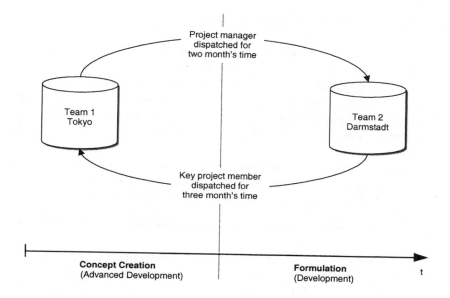

Fig. 53. Know-how travels with heads at Kao.

ment was carried out in regional R&D centers. Fig. 53 depicts this concept in an example of hair treatment development in Tokyo and Darmstadt.

Know-how between Japanese advanced development and German development was transferred by mutual personnel exchange. First, a German scientist was sent to Tokyo for three months to take part in the concept creation with the local project team. During the development in Darmstadt, the Japanese project manager supported the German team for two months. In this case, personnel continuity ensured technology transfer.

Conclusions

Managers of pharmaceutical R&D are confronted by increased pressure regarding improvements in the number of new drugs and their respective clinical profiles, as well as concerns over cost reductions and speed in the R&D process. Key success factors for meeting these challenges are: to have the right people in the right organization working on the right projects. Escalating R&D costs are compensated by increased outsourcing of non-core activities and a clear concentration on commercial activities.

Balancing R&D and Commercialization

Pfizer is known to be the most successful pharmaceutical company worldwide. However, comparing R&D-to-sales ratios, other pharmaceutical companies can claim to be more innovative than Pfizer. Pfizer's number one position seems to be based on its higher spending on sales support and marketing. Most other companies focus more narrowly on research and development.

To be successful in the pharmaceutical market it is important to establish a balanced combination and alignment of R&D and sales. The goal of any pharmaceutical company should be to be as strong in marketing and sales as in research and development.

Effective knowledge management becomes more important. Knowledge is no longer restricted to research, such as information on active substances, but also includes knowledge about the important players in the scientific community as well as knowledge about potential cooperation partners or acquisition candidates in the early innovation phase. The most efficient knowledge transfer mechanism of complex know-how is through moving people: Know-how travels with heads. Blueprints are not enough. Job rotation promotes transfer of tacit knowledge.

In the increasingly complex project environment, expertise is no longer sufficient for successful project management. Instead, professionalism in project management is a must for pharmaceutical companies. Companies are trying to meet this challenge with project oriented incentive systems (e.g., dual career ladders), strong project organizations (e.g., heavy-weight-project-manager), and virtual project manager pools (e.g., Roche).

Managing the entire portfolio of different projects at various stages of the product pipeline is the key to successful R&D management. A clear focus on each project's commercial potential requires the establishment of a business-oriented mindset throughout the entire pipeline including the early research and discovery stages. Human resource activities are becoming increasingly critical. Strong motivation, clear incentive systems and a culture that supports innovation are a necessity.

VII. Future Directions and Trends

> *„When it comes to R&D, we must recognize that many of the good opportunities have been picked off already and that the new opportunities are increasingly hard to find and very risky. This will be perhaps the biggest challenge for our industry in sustaining product flow."*
>
> Fred Hassan,
> *then CEO at Pharmacia, 2002*

Closing the productivity gap in research and development is the foremost task in the pharmaceutical industry and represents the single-most important direction for future activities in pharmaceutical innovation. The pharmaceutical industry is facing a great number of challenges. This final chapter identifies some trends and suggests potential future directions in leading pharmaceutical innovation:

- There will be fewer and fewer companies with more and more blockbusters in the future. Also, it is expected that diseases will become increasingly more complex to treat. Hence, it is important to contemplate if the traditional paradigm of the blockbuster concept is still applicable for treating or preventing the more complex diseases. Pharmaceutical companies will not be able to rely on a few blockbuster products anymore. Personalized medicine, dependant on the genetic profiles of the patients, is required. However, people share about 99% identical DNA; the remaining 1% of differing DNA provides the opportunity for tailor-made drugs. Existing products could then be customized. Economic consequences of the resulting patient segmentation and product customization have to be considered. New business models are required as well. For example, even a single compound can then create its own market.
- A stronger market-orientation in R&D is one of the primary tasks for future R&D activities. This in turn requires a stronger business orientation of research managers and key scientists. Many scientists in pharmaceutical R&D still know too little about the markets which their prod-

ucts are expected to serve. A clear communication of the business benefits to the scientists is necessary. As a consequence, an effective and collaborative interface between R&D and marketing must be established. Ultimately, a stronger market-orientation is expected to result in a shift from a product- to a patient-driven strategy.

- The quality of the product pipeline has to be constantly improved while the volatility of the product pipeline has to be reduced. Genuinely innovative products have a higher potential to deliver growth and shareholder value than patent defense of existing products. In addition, volatility in new product releases has a direct impact on the overall cost of capital of the corporation.

- The more we understand the human genome, the more validated biological targets will be available that will be starting points for new drug development. It is expected that the number of targets will increase by a factor of more than 20 to over 10'000 targets by 2007.

- In addition, the integration of genomics, proteomics, molecular design, and other technologies will lead to improved target identification and attrition, enhanced lead optimization, improved clinical trial designs that speed approval, and signal a shift from broadly targeted drugs to more focused medicines with much higher therapeutic value for the target population. With access to genomics technologies estimated to require a minimum US$ 100 million annual commitment, top-tier pharmaceutical companies are likely to be the first to fully integrate the new technologies.

- A wide range of other novel drug discovery technologies already in use, such as high-throughput screening, combinatorial chemistry, bioinformatics, and molecular drug design are expected to improve pharmaceutical research as well. The application of these technologies allows for the automation of much of the discovery function, promoting a more comprehensive and consistent screening process as well as enhancements in R&D productivity. This means a move away from a disease-centered to a systematic and mechanistic discovery process in the early phases. As a result, both the quality and quantity of resulting lead compounds are expected to increase.

- Besides applying more advanced screening methodologies, the quality of the substances that are to be screened also has to improve. Therefore, the structural complexity and diversity of the compound libraries must increase. This ultimately allows to raise the probability to find a substance that is able to influence a certain target in the desired way.

- The increasing deployment of information technologies has resulted in huge amounts of data being generated day-by-day. After the development of new information production techniques new information management techniques are required. Advanced database technologies, faster algorithms and improved statistical analyses are necessary to efficiently screen through vast quantities of information possibly eliminating at some point the reliance on serendipity alone for future successes.

- People are at the center of any organization, thus improved people development and training will result in better run companies. Pharmaceutical companies will have to overcome the distance between early-stage research and the final product by adapting their incentive and job assignment systems. Not every scientist wants to do a stint in marketing, but every researcher should have had the exposure to the rest of the business and the opportunity to pursue a less traditional career.

- An oftentimes mentioned concern in pharmaceutical R&D is the fact that people do not interact enough with each other. Modern drug discovery requires the integration of knowledge from a broad array of disciplines. The formation of multidisciplinary teams, including biologists, physiologists, biochemists, as well as specialists in the traditional disciplines of synthetic chemistry and pharmacology, and more esoteric specialists like molecular kineticists is a necessity. In addition, marketing experts should always be included at every stage of the R&D process. The most successful pharmaceutical companies differentiate themselves by actively confronting the tension between an organization by function and an organization by product group.

- Every employee in the R&D department should ask themselves what their contribution could be across all levels of the R&D process. This approach should eliminate the linear structured process and move towards more group- and team-oriented R&D. Feedback loops (i.e., from the clinical trials back to basic research and the screening stages) must be proactively pursued.

- It has been shown that creativity in pharmaceutical R&D is most likely to occur in smaller teams. The trend towards mega-mergers and ever larger companies is endangering R&D's ability to be creative. Hence, with any acquisition and/or integration of outside knowledge into the inside portfolio, which is expected to be a major driver for improvement in R&D in the future, there is the potential loss of creativity and the occurrence of the not-invented-here syndrome. Embedded small functional units within the larger unit are expected to be a successful approach against these negative consequences.

- Fail often to succeed sooner. It is more economical and productive to terminate less prospective projects and concentrate resources on objectively more promising ones. There is a cut-off after which project management gives discipline absolute priority over incremental improvements. Before this cut-off, the R&D organization should be designed for maximal creativity and effectiveness of its discovery effort. Overall, the combined thrust of all project activities determines a company's competence areas and thus therapeutic fields.

- Reduced efficiency and flexibility, difficulties to transfer know-how and an unclear intellectual property situation are seen as major disadvantages in pharmaceutical R&D. Service providers, which could complement the competencies of the pharmaceutical company, may take over an increasingly important role in managing pharmaceutical innovation. Regarding the pharmaceutical company, the balance between in-house and external activities (make-or-buy decision) is mostly competency or know-how driven and not capacity or cost driven. Preferred partnerships and cooperation on a project-by-project basis with pre-selected vendors are the two most favorable cooperation models in practice. However, controlling the critical components in the value chain remains an important issue.

- Pharmaceutical products are ideally global. Hence, R&D has also to adopt an increasingly internationalized strategy. Foremost, it is important to align the R&D strategy with corporate strategy. Is global R&D a consequence of business decisions, or is global business a consequence of R&D decisions? In this regard, it is essential to clarify what decision criteria exist and which criteria would influence the initial mission, ramp-up and evaluation of new R&D sites. Company-wide knowledge management and information and communication technologies play a critical role in the overall internationalization process.

R&D of pharmaceutical companies has been facing intense criticism due to declining productivity. The pharmaceutical industry relies on predictable production of new medicines and therapies. While we have found many threats and dangers that imperil the prospects of any single company, the overall industry is looking forward to an exciting future. Several new technologies in the drug discovery process are in their infancy and are expected to revolutionize the way pharmaceutical companies manage innovation. The incorporation of market-oriented aspects, improved human resource and project leadership, better R&D pipeline management, and a balanced outsourcing and internationalization strategy, are major elements in a general strategy towards success. The pharmaceutical company of the future is expected to move away from treating illness to pursuing a vision of managing wellness.

VIII. Appendices

Case: R&D Management at Novartis

Novartis was formed in 1996 through the merger of Ciba Geigy and Sandoz. Cost savings from the merger have resulted in net profit margins at the high end of the industry average; this has enabled Novartis to invest significantly in organic growth. In addition, Novartis consolidated activities with the divestment of non-core businesses. As a first and significant step, the company spun-off its CHF 8 billion specialty chemicals business Ciba SC in 1997. Afterwards, Novartis divested its CHF 5.5 billion agribusiness sector, merging it with the agrochemicals business of Astra-Zeneca to form Syngenta. Novartis now operates its core businesses in two divisions: pharmaceuticals and consumer health.

The company's product portfolio in pharmaceuticals includes a range of products in seven major disease areas: cardiovascular/metabolism/endocrinology; oncology/hematology; central nervous system; transplantation/immunology; respiratory/dermatology; rheumatology/bone/hormone replacement therapy/gastrointestinal and ophthalmics. The pharmaceuticals division is organized into five business units: primary care, oncology, transplantation, ophthalmics and mature products. The product portfolio includes more than 30 key marketed products, of which four were launched in 2002. In addition, the portfolio includes more than 60 potential products or potential additional indications for existing products in various stages of development.

The consumer health division covers generics, over-the-counter (OTC) self-medication, animal health, medical nutrition, infant and baby foods and products, as well as eyecare products. In November 2002, the company completed the divestment of its food and beverage business, including Ovaltine/Ovomaltine, Caotina and Lacovo, to Associated British Foods. The remaining health and functional food businesses, the Health Food & Slimming and Sports Nutrition lines, have been re-organized into a stand-alone unit called Nutrition et Sante, headquartered in France.

The business of Novartis' generics business unit is conducted by a number of affiliated companies worldwide. In 2003, the Company announced plans to unite 14 of the generics company brands under a single global umbrella name, Sandoz. The goal was to strengthen recognition and leverage share of voice in the highly competitive marketplace for generics products. The affiliated companies of the generics business unit compete in three principal product segments: finished dosage forms (generic pharmaceuticals business), active pharmaceutical ingredients and their intermediates (industrial business), and biopharmaceuticals (biopharmaceuticals business).

Key to Novartis' growth strategy will be the efforts to increase the firm's presence in the US, the largest market globally and accounting for the largest share of the company's pharmaceutical sales. Novartis has almost doubled the size of its US sales force since 1998, and now has a US sales team of close to 5'000 sales representatives. In addition, in 2002 Novartis announced the launch of a corporate 'Institute for BioMedical Research' in Cambridge/Massachussetts, directly located beside MIT, which is supposed to take the lead in worldwide corporate R&D activities. However, Novartis' presence in the US market is still in need of improvement. According to Reuters (2002), Novartis will struggle to maintain double-digit growth in ethical sales in the long term despite a promising pipeline and launch schedule over the next three years due to the company's relatively weak position in the US. A merger might be a conceivable solution, and Roche has been cited as a potential partner although Roche would not offer the significant geographical benefits needed for Novartis.

Still, Novartis raised its stake in Roche in January 2003, setting the stage for an eventual takeover of its rival. According to the Wall Street Journal, the move came as a shock to Roche, which viewed it as a hardball tactic by Novartis to force the Hoffmann and Oeri families, which control 50.1% of the voting shares, to sell out. By holding 32.7% of Roche's voting shares, up from 21.3%, Novartis essentially gains veto power over any of strategic move Roche might try to make. Novartis spent about CHF 2.9 billion for the new shares.

In May 2003, Novartis acquired Idenix Pharmaceuticals, a biopharmaceutical company engaged in the discovery and development of drugs for the treatment of human viral and other infectious diseases. Also in May 2003, the company acquired the incontinence drug Enablex from Pfizer. In 2000, Novartis completed the acquisition of the antiviral products Famvir (famciclovir) and Vectavir/Denavir (penciclovir) from SmithKline Beecham.

Key figures

In 2002, Novartis achieved sales of CHF 32.4 billion and a net income of CHF 7.3 billion. The group invested approximately CHF 4.3 billion in R&D, resulting in a R&D-to-sales ratio of 13.2% for the entire group. Only the pharmaceutical division reported a R&D-to-sales ratio of 17.1% in 2001. Headquartered in Basel, Switzerland, Novartis employs about 72'900 people worldwide and operates in over 140 countries around the globe. In 2002, Novartis reported a profit margin of 22.6%, which was significantly higher than the average profit margin of the 16 leading pharmaceutical companies.

Pharmaceuticals accounted for 65% of 2002 revenues, which is equivalent to CHF 21.0 billion. Consumer health products, which includes such brands as Gerber baby foods, ExLax, Maalox, Tavist, and Theraflu, accounted for the remaining 35% of sales. Out of the total sales, 43% were recorded in the USA, 33% in Europe, 17% in Africa/Asia/Australia and 7% in the rest of the Americas.

The core pharmaceuticals business posted double-digit sales growth in 2002, gaining total market share during the year. Overall, sales grew 13% (4% in CHF) over the full year. In the US market, sales grew 12%. Double-digit sales growth was also achieved in all other major regions. In Europe, strong volume gains in Spain and France offset the effects of pricing pressures in several countries.

Sales growth has primarily been due to the key therapy areas cardiovascular and oncology. The best selling cardiovascular products include the hypertensive products Diovan and Lotrel, and the cholesterol reduction product Lescol. The most successful products in oncology are Gleevec against chronic myelogenous leukemia, Zometa against cancer-related bone complications as well as Sandostatin for the treatment of acromegaly, carcinoid syndrome.

Research & development

Novartis has a solid history of successful drug discovery and one of the best pipelines in the industry. In 2001 and 2002, Novartis achieved the highest number of key-market approvals in the pharmaceutical industry, with 20 registrations and 22 major submissions in the United States, the European Union and Japan. As measured by the number of new product approvals, Novartis was the most effective generator of innovation quality worldwide in 2000 and 2001. Novartis introduced 5 new products in 2000 and 4 new products in 2001. Novartis' investment in new genomics alliances and partnerships has also resulted in a significant number of new targets, technologies and pipeline projects. In total, Novartis owns 172 patents (Reuters 2002). Novartis has successfully launched a number of high profile products in the US, including Gleevec and Zometa for cancer patients, Elidel for eczema and Zelmac/Zelnorm for irritable bowel syndrome, further rejuvenating the product portfolio.

With a steady flow of development compounds, the product pipeline is under constant review and comprises a total of 67 projects in clinical development as of October 2002. This includes both new molecular entities and additional indications or formulations for marketed products. Overall, there are 30 projects in late-stage development (Phase III/regulatory), to sustain mid-term growth, and a substantial number of projects (25) in Phase II. To increase R&D capacity and strengthen the skill base, more than 1'000 research scientists and associates have been added over the past two years, with plans to add another 1'000 employees in the foreseeable future.

Novartis deploys several research centers worldwide, which can be classified to one of the following two research institute groups:

- Novartis Institutes for BioMedical Research;
- Novartis Corporate Research Institutes.

Pharmaceutical research is primarily conducted through the Novartis Institutes for BioMedical Research, led by Mark Fishman, professor at the Harvard Medical School. The Novartis Institutes for BioMedical Research are headquartered in Cambridge, Massachusetts, and have several locations around the world. The Cambridge facility currently houses over 400 scientists and technology experts and is expected to expand to approximately 1'000 employees in the near future. The Cambridge headquarters will continue to grow, with a US$ 4 billion investment planned over the next 10 years. Aligned with the corporate world headquarters, Novartis Institutes in Basel are an integral part of the BioValley, Europe's biotechnology hub. This research facility houses approximately 1'500 temporary and permanent research associates. The other main Novartis Research Institutes are located in East Hanover (US), Horsham (UK, focus on respiratory disease), Vienna (AU, focus on dermatology), Tsukuba (JP, focus on arthritis), and London (UK, focus on pain).

The Novartis Corporate Research Institutes, headed by Paul Herrling, have a different mission than the Novartis Institutes for BioMedical Research. The Friedrich Miescher Institute in Basel performs basic research in areas of wider interest to Novartis Pharma. The Novartis Institute for Tropical Diseases in Singapore (under construction) aims to develop drugs against neglected diseases like dengue fever and tuberculosis. The Genomics Institute of the Novartis Research Foundation in La Jolla, California, searches for and characterizes new drug targets that could potentially be included in the pharmaceutical pipeline.

According to Savioz (2002), all R&D activities at Novartis are fully decentralized to sectors. R&D at Novartis Pharma is organized by a matrix of three dimensions: therapeutic areas, core technologies and senior experts. Those responsible for general coordination of these three R&D dimension meet monthly as the Research Management Board, consisting of heads of therapeutic areas, heads of core technologies, senior experts and the head of research. Project decisions, in particular rough resource allocation, are the main focus of this board meeting. However, therapeutic areas and core technologies are quite independent of strategic planning and 'detailed' resource allocation. Thus, this is a bottom-up process that is 'controlled' by an upper level. R&D activities within these three dimensions are dispersed among several global research centers, mainly in Europe and the USA. Besides internal R&D activities, Novartis Pharma maintains a cooperation network. At the group level a central 'Group Technology' coordinates the sector's technology strategies, detects synergy potentials, and is responsible for knowledge management and generation of new businesses. This group is supported by two scientific advisory boards, the Research Advisory Board for product technology purposes and the Technology Advisory Board for process technology purposes, which include, among other members, the key heads of R&D and production. In summary, the most important characteristics of R&D and technology management are:

- Decentralized sectors and therefore very international R&D;
- Projects that are financed by sectors, some budgets for new technologies at the group level;
- Participative planning in sectors, coordination of synergies at the group level;
- Science-based and technology-driven business;
- Market-driven innovation culture as well as bottom-up-driven decision-making culture.

Development and marketing are integrated into discovery at start of product continuum and are an important part of research portfolio reviews. Novartis relies on multidisciplinary groups of researchers to solve target structures and focus on designing drugs rationally. This reduces the number of compounds that are tested to find a successful one. Groups are divided into four general sections – structured bioinformatics, molecular modeling, protein expression and purification, and those that perform structural biology work – these groups work in collaboration rather than sitting in specialized groups.

Strategic alliances

Novartis invests around 30% of its research budget in external collaborations. So far, these collaborations have delivered 37 pipeline projects, more than 40 novel targets and 12 new technologies (Reuters 2002). Recent alliance agreements both regarding research and development are listed in the following tables.

Table 16. Major research alliances at Novartis.

Partner	Activities
Friedrich Miescher Institute, Basel, Switzerland	Broad-based research
Scripps Research Institute, La Jolla, USA	Broad-based research
Celera, Rockville, USA	Functional genomics, gene databases
Incyte Genomics, Palo Alto, USA	Functional genomics, LifeSeq databases, gene chips
GeneProt, Geneva, Switzerland	Proteomics
Rigel, Sunnyvale, USA	Functional genomics, target discovery and validation
SNP Consortium	Functional genomics, SNPs map
GeneData, Basel, Switzerland	Functional genomics, gene expression analysis
Celgene, New Jersey, USA	Osteoporosis, selective estrogen receptor modulator compounds
University of Vienna, Austria	Dermatology, dendritic cells
Maryland Psychiatric Research Center, USA	Nervous system, proteomics, schizophrenia
Neuroscience Center Zurich, Switzerland	Neurosciences
Avant Immunotherapeutics	Transplantation, complement inhibitor TP10
Yoshitomi, Japan	Transplantation, FTY 720 immunosuppresant

Table 16. (continued).

Cubist, Lexington, USA	Infectious diseases
Versicor, Fremont, USA	Infectious diseases
Dana Farber Cancer Institute	Oncology, signal transduction
Xenogen, Alameda, USA	Oncology, imaging technology
Biozentrum, Basel, Switzerland	Nuclear magnetic resonance technology
LifeSpan, USA	G-protein-coupled receptors
Medarex, Princeton, USA	Human monoclonal antibody technology
Vertex, USA	Kinases
Cytos, Zurich, Switzerland	Therapeutic Vaccine Technology

Source: Novartis (2003)

Besides research alliances, Novartis has also signed several development partnerships as listed in the following table.

Table 17. Major development alliances at Novartis.

Partner	Activities
Regeneron Pharmaceuticals, New York, USA	Rheumatoid arthritis
Idenix Pharmaceuticals, Cambridge, USA	Antiviral
Elan, Dublin, Ireland	Drug delivery
Emisphere Technologies, Tarrytown, USA	Drug delivery
SkyePharma, London, UK	Drug delivery
Lohmann	Drug delivery
Noven, Miami, USA	Drug delivery

Table 17. (continued).

Biosite, Täby, Sweden	Bioassay
Speedel, Basel, Switzerland	Cardiovascular, hypertension
Sibia, USA/Merck	Nervous system, epilepsy
Knoll	Nervous system, schizophrenia
Titan Pharmaceuticals, San Francisco, USA	Nervous system, schizophrenia
Celgene, Warren, USA	Nervous system, ADHD
Orion, Espoo, Finland	Nervous system, Parkinson's disease
Dainippon, Osaka, Japan	Nervous system, anxiety
Genentech/Tanox	Allergy, asthma
Schering, Berlin, Germany	Oncology, angiogenesis
Ajinomoto, Japan	Diabetes
Dr. Reddy, Hyderabad, India	Diabetes
QLT, Vancouver, Canada	Ophthalmology and oncology

Source: Novartis (2003)

Novartis has one central research location in Tokyo. Additionally, the 'Novartis Foundation Japan for the Promotion of Science' was founded by predecessor Ciba in 1987. The foundation contributes to the improvement of mankind's welfare, by aiding and promoting creative research and pursuing international exchange among researchers in the field of biological and medical sciences, and related chemistry.

As part of the foundation's activities, Novartis provides research grants, and grants for a Japan-Europe scientific exchange program and for international research meetings. The activities of the foundation include:

- Aiding creative research in the field of natural sciences;
- Aiding international exchanges among researchers involved in creative research in the field of natural sciences;

- Sponsoring and/or supporting meetings of various academic societies and research workshops relating to creative research in the field of natural sciences;
- Publishing and/or aiding in the publication of books and periodicals concerning the promotion of creative research in the field of natural sciences.

Case: R&D Management at Roche

Roche develops, manufactures and markets high-quality products and services in the field of healthcare. The company focuses its activities on the prevention, diagnosis and treatment of diseases and on the promotion of general well-being. Roche markets and sells its pharmaceutical products through its own subsidiaries in more than 50 countries and through local partners in other countries. The group has significantly restructured its business activities over the past few years. In 2002, Roche sold its vitamins and fine chemicals division to DSM in the Netherlands. Roche operates now two divisions: pharmaceuticals and diagnostics.

More than 140 subsidiaries worldwide belong to the Roche Group. The company Hoffmann-La Roche is the US prescription pharmaceuticals unit of the Roche Group. The company takes its name from its Swiss founder, Fritz Hoffmann-La Roche. Descendents of the founding Hoffmann and Oeri families own a significant stake of Roche. The Roche subsidiary develops and makes drugs to treat such life-threatening conditions as AIDS, cancer, and heart disease. The company also provides treatments for central nervous system and mental disorders, influenza, and obesity. Roche's prescription drugs include antibiotic Rocephin; obesity treatment Xenical; AIDS drug Invirase; acne medication Roaccutan/Accutane; and Tamiflu, which is used to prevent and treat influenza. Roche has invested heavily in diagnostics, including advanced DNA tests, to become one of the top companies in the diagnostics field.

In 2002, Roche reinforced its position as the world leader in oncology. Oncology, the largest and fastest-growing therapeutic area, now accounts for nearly one third of total prescription drug sales. The innovative products leading the oncology portfolio, MabThera/Rituxan, Herceptin and Xeloda, have only been on the market for a few years, and all three have been shown to extend patient survival. In 2001, Roche expanded its strong oncology pipeline through alliances with companies such as Antisoma, Kosan and Beaufour Ipsen.

Over the next five years Roche plans to file up to 29 new drug applications in key therapeutic areas such as oncology, HIV/AIDS and anxiety/depression. The company intends to additionally strengthen its portfolio by continuing its intensive in-licensing activities.

Roche owns almost 60% of the biotechnology firm Genentech. Additionally, Roche acquired Japan's Chugai Pharmaceutical in 2002. The merger of Nippon Roche and Chugai has created the fifth-largest pharmaceuticals company and the fourth-largest sales force in Japan. This provides powerful leverage for existing and future Roche products in this key market. Moreover, Chugai now has one of the biggest development organizations in Japan, a factor that will help Roche to develop and launch products faster in the coming years.

Key figures

Roche generated revenues of CHF 29.7 billion in 2002 and posted a loss of CHF 4.0 billion due to substantial one-time charges, such as litigation payments, impairment charges, and investment losses. However, the group's EBITDA was solid with CHF 6.0 billion. Roche invested approximately CHF 4.2 billion in R&D, resulting in a R&D-to-sales ratio of 14.1% for the entire group. Only the pharmaceutical division reported a R&D-to-sales ratio of 17.6%. Headquartered in Basel, Switzerland, Roche employs about 69'700 people worldwide.

The pharmaceutical division accounted for 65% of revenues in 2002, which is equivalent to CHF 19.3 billion. Diagnostics accounted for about 24% of sales or CHF 7.2 billion respectively. The remaining amount is due to sales of vitamins, fine chemicals, fragrances and flavors, which were divested in 2002. Adjusted by the divestments, Roche's total sales figure would be CHF 26.5 billion instead of CHF 29.7 billion in 2002. The pharmaceutical division is said to remain committed to raising its operating profit margin towards 25% in the next two years.

The pharmaceutical division's prescription drug sales cover the following therapeutic areas including their respective contribution to total pharmaceutical sales: oncology (29%), metabolic disorders (10%), infectious disease (10%), cardiovascular disease (9%), central nervous system (8%), virology (7%), transplantation (7%), dermatology (6%), anemia (5%), inflammatory disease/bone (3%), and others (6%).

The majority of drugs were sold in North America, with 41% of total prescription drug sales, whereas Europe comes in second with 33%. Japan was responsible for 9%, with Latin America accounting for 8% of prescription drug sales.

Research & development

Roche's research is based on a distinctive innovation model and a clear strategy in which partnerships play a key role. Apart from Roche's own powerful in-house research organization, the pharmaceuticals division's R&D network also includes Genentech and Chugai, which function as largely independent research satellites. In addition, Roche has opt-in rights to the programs of external development organizations it has created, such as BioXell, set up in 2002, and Basilea Pharmaceutica. This is a further source of promising compounds for the company's product pipeline. With 25 agreements concluded with other companies last year, Roche now ranks among the industry leaders in terms of licensing. In total, the Roche Group owns 166 patents (Reuters 2002).

As of January 2003, Roche is pursuing 135 pharmaceutical research projects in-house (see Table 18). In 2002, 12 new molecular entities entered phase 0, and 7 entered phase I clinical testing. The pharmaceuticals division currently has 65 new molecular entities in its development pipeline. This includes opt-in opportunities (9), potential new medicines that Genentech will develop (6) and Chugai projects (10). Roche has the right to license-in any projects for which Chugai seeks a partner outside Japan and South Korea. The increased number of promising new molecular entities compared with 2001 is a result of structural adjustments in the pharmaceutical R&D organization. The number of projects in phase II development has increased significantly during the past two years. The seamless R&D process which Roche has established in recent years promotes better decision-making and thus contributes to creating greater future value. Ongoing initiatives are concentrating on further optimizing productivity, with the focus more on the value generated by each project than on quantity. Progress has been achieved by implementing a number of tools for com-

Table 18. R&D pipeline of Roche in January 2003.

Area of Focus	Number of Projects
Central nervous system	24
Genitourinary diseases	9
Inflammatory diseases	17
Metabolic diseases	30
Oncology	37
Vascular diseases	8
Virology	10
Total	**135**

Source: Roche (2003)

pound selection and profiling at the early research stage. These have been harmonized across all research centers.

At Roche, the research and development organizations are separated and organized in different ways. On the one hand, research is performed at four major research sites (see Table 19); each site acts as a center of excellence for certain disease areas. On the other hand, development is globally coordinated with the project leaders located in different areas, mainly at the same sites as the research activities.

Additionally, research and development have different organizational structures. Research is organized to allow innovation and maintain a certain degree of freedom necessary for the creativity of scientists in research. Development is focused on the management task of bringing drug candidates to market as quickly and efficiently as possible.

The present geographical research site configuration is in place mainly for historical reasons. The Basel site evolved from Roche's classical research areas such as bacteriology, central nervous system and cardiovascular disease. Metabolic disease and autoimmune disease were established from the beginning in the US.

Table 19. R&D sites and designated research areas at Roche.

Sites	Research Areas
Basel, Switzerland	Metabolic disorders
	Central nervous system
	Vascular disease
Nutley, USA	Metabolic disorders
	Oncology
	Vascular disease
Palo Alto, USA	Central nervous system
	Inflammatory disease/bone
	Genitourinary disease
	Viral disease
Penzberg, Germany	Oncology

Source: Roche (2003)

Each center has a certain technology in which it excels and offers this technology as a service to the other centers. Nutley, for example, has extensive knowledge in the genomics area through close links with specialized biotechnology companies such as Millennium.

Development is globally coordinated with a Project Development Meeting responsible for the entire steering of drug development. Projects are developed according to the requirements of the key countries of market interest which are the USA, Japan and the major European markets. An International Project Team is the key organizational group for developing prescription medicines. An international project manager leading the International Project Team is usually located at the site where most of the research leading to the development project takes place.

Strategic alliances

The pharmaceutical division of the Roche Group has entered several strategic alliances for multiple purposes. The most important alliances are listed in the following table.

Table 20. Strategic alliances at Roche.

Partner	Activities
Affymetrix	Supplies DNA probe arrays for use in Roche's research and development activities. Chip technology aids the identification of genes that are expressed at different levels in healthy and diseased tissue.
Agouron	Viracept Protease Inhibitor.
Anadys	Drug discovery collaboration to advance lead compounds identified by Roche against an important oncology target.
Antisoma	Broad strategic alliance granting Roche exclusive worldwide rights to the Antisoma pipeline of oncology products.
Beaufour-Ipsen	Co-development and marketing agreement of oncology products.
BioFocus	Manufacturing of compounds to extend Roche's library.
Biovation	Use of deimmunisation technology to generate novel biopharmaceuticals.
Cardion	License to human Interleukin IL-15 Cytokine Receptor Blocker for autoimmune diseases.
DeCODE	Aimed at building on the achievements of the previous gene discovery collaboration by using the targets identified to discover and develop new therapeutic compounds in a drug discovery program.
ETH	Bio NMR research support.
Evotec OAI	Development of chemical libraries for inclusion into Roche compound repository.
Genmab	Production of therapeutic antibodies to select novel targets.
Gilead	Influenza neuraminidase inhibitors.

Table 20. (continued).

Gryphon	Development of Synthetic Erythropoiesis Protein (SEP) for the treatment of common conditions which cause anemia.
GSK	Co-development and co-promotion of Bonviva for the treatment of osteoporosis.
Isotechnika	Co-development of ISATX247 in organ transplantation and in the treatment for autoimmune diseases.
Karolinska	Gene expression patterns in obese patients (new target identification).
Kosan Biosciences	Co-development and co-commercialization of Kosan's anti-cancer drug candidate KOS-862 (Epothilone D).
Max Planck Society	Sponsoring of Research Groups in the fields of Apoptosis, Cell Cycle, Bone Development.
Max Planck Institute of Biochemistry	X-Ray Structural Analysis / Crystallography.
Maxygen	Global development and commercialization of Maxygen's portfolio of next generation interferon alpha and beta variants for the treatment of Hepatitis C and a number of other indications.
Maybridge	Development of chemical libraries for inclusion into Roche compound repository.
Medivir	Development of a non-nucleoside reverse transcriptase inhibitor (NNRTI) in HIV treatment.
Memory	Development of compounds for Alzheimer's disease and other neurological indications.
MorphoSys	Alzheimer's disease: Humanised monoclonal antibodies.
Norak	Use of Norak's Transfluor™ technology as a high-throughput screening (HTS) assay to discover G protein-coupled receptor active compounds.
OSI	Co-development and commercialization of the anti-cancer compound Tarceva.
Partners Healthcare	Establishment of DNA laboratory in order to combine genotypic and phenotypic data, for the extension of scientific knowledge in the genetic causes of disease and to facilitate diagnosis and therapy of disease.
PheneX	Research technology collaboration.
Ribapharm	Development of Levovirin for the treatment of Hepatitis C.
Royal Free Hospital, UCL	Development of a new drug for Amyloidosis.

Table 20. (continued).

Specs	Compound supply for chemical library.
Stressgen Bio-technologies	Co-development and commercialization of HspE7 for Human Papilloma Virus diseases.
Telik	Chemical fingerprinting for CRF-1 receptor antagonists.
Trimeris	HIV: anti-HIV peptide fusion peptides.
Tularik	Inflammation drug discovery.
Vernalis	Collaboration on the research and development of 5HT2c receptor agonists for treatment of obesity, novel drugs for the treatment of diabetes.

Source: Roche (2003)

In addition to the alliances in the pharmaceutical area, Roche has entered into 57 strategic alliances with biotechnology firms (Lin 2001). The most notable collaboration with a biotechnology company is Roche's 60% stake in Genentech.

The most notable activity of Roche in the Japanese market is the acquisition of Chugai Pharmaceutical. Named 'Chugai, a member of the Roche Group', the new company will be Roche's exclusive pharmaceutical representative in Japan and will have rights to develop and market all pharmaceutical products which the Roche Group decides to commercialize in Japan. Roche will have the right to license-in all Chugai products outside of Japan and South Korea for which Chugai seeks a partner.

The combined activities have led Roche to become the fifth largest pharmaceutical company in Japan, right after Takeda, Sankyo, Yamanouchi and Daiichi. Due to the acquisition, Roche's total sales of prescription drugs in Japan increased to about JPY 200 billion, which is equivalent to about CHF 2.5 billion. This accounts for about 19% of Roche's total pharmaceutical sales. Prior to the acquisition, the Japanese market accounted only for 6% of Roche's pharmaceutical sales.

Bibliography

Accenture (2001a): High Performance Drug Discovery – An Operating Model for a New Era. Executive Briefing. Accenture Report.

Accenture (2001b): R&D and the Internet. Accenture Report.

Albers, S.; Eggers, S. (1991): Organisatorische Gestaltungen von Produktinnovations-Prozessen. Führt der Wechsel des Organisationsgrades zu Innovationserfolg? Zeitschrift für Betriebswirtschaftliche Forschung, Vol. 43, Iss. 1, pp. 44-64.

Arthur D. Little (2003): Aktuelle Trends bei Buyouts in der Chemie- und Pharmaindustrie. Market Study, January 2003.

Arthur D. Little, Solvias (2002): External Synthesis Services for Research and Development in the Pharmaceutical Industry. Market Study, June 2002.

Agarwal, S.; Desai, S.; Holcomb, M.M.; Oberoi, A. (2001): Unlocking the Value in Big Pharma. The McKinsey Quarterly, 2001, No. 2.

BAK (2001): Garant und Motor für Produktivität und Wohlstand in der Schweiz – Bedeutung der chemisch/pharmazeutischen Industrie für die Schweizer Volkswirtschaft. Baseler Konjunkturforschung: Basel.

Baumann (2003): The Challenge of Innovation in the Drug Discovery Process. Presentation at CTO-Roundtable 'Management of Pharmaceutical R&D in Turbulent Times – Perspectives and Trends'. Zurich, March 2003.

BCG (2001): A Revolution in R&D – How Genomics and Genetics are Transforming the Biopharmaceutical Industry. BCG Report: Boston MA.

Booz Allen & Hamilton (1997): In Vivo, Making Combinatory Chemistry Pay. Booz Allen & Hamilton Report: New York.

Boutellier, R.; Gassmann, O.; von Zedtwitz, M. (1999): Managing Global Innovation: Uncovering the Secrets of Future Competitiveness. 2nd ed., Springer: Berlin, Tokyo, New York.

BPI (1999): Die 'Innovationsschere' der pharmazeutischen Industrie. Taken from Prof. Homburg & Partner (2001): Trends und Chancen in der Pharma-Branche. Mannheim, April 2001.

Buderi, R; Weber, J.; Hoots, C.; Neff, R. (1991): A Tighter Focus for R&D. Business Week, 2 December 1991, pp. 80-84.

Budworth, D.W. (1996): Finance and Innovation. New York.

Cantwell, J. (1995): The Globalisation of Technology: What Remains of the Product Cycle Model? In: Cambridge Journal of Economics, Vol. 19, pp. 155-174.

CDER (2002): Center for Drug Evaluation and Research at FDA: http://www.fda.gov/cder/, accessed September 2002.

Chesbrough, H. (2003): Open Innovation: The New Imperative for Creating and Profiting from Technology. Harvard Business School Press: Boston MA.

Dalton, D.H.; Serapio, M.G. (1995): Globalizing Industrial Research and Development. Washington D.C.: U.S. Department of Commerce.

Davis, S.; Botkin, J. (1994): The Coming of Knowledge-Based Business. Harvard Business Review, 5, pp. 165-170.

De Meyer, A. (1991): Tech Talk: How Managers Are Stimulating Global R&D Communication. Sloan Management Review, 32, 3, pp. 49-58.

DiMasi, J. (2001): Tufts Center for the Study of Drug Development Pegs Costs of a New Prescription Drug at $802 Million. Press release, Tufts University, 30 November 2001.

Economiesuisse (2002): F+E in der Schweizerischen Privatwirtschaft. Zürich.

Ernst&Young (2002): Beyond Borders – The Global Biotechnology Report 2002. Global Health Sciences. Ernst&Young Report.

Federal Social Insurance Office (2002): http://www.bsv.admin.ch/, accessed September 2002.

Federal Statistical Office (1998): Costs of Public Health Care. Bern. http://www.statistik.admin.ch/, accessed September 2002.

Federal Statistical Office (1999): Costs of Public Health Care. Bern. http://www.statistik.admin.ch/, accessed February 2003.

Festel, G.; Polastro, E. (2002): Dritte arbeiten häufig kostengünstiger. Chemische Rundschau, Vol. 55, No. 13, 28 June 2002, p. 7.

Freudenheim, M.; Peterson, M. (2001): The Drug-Price Express Runs into a Wall. The New York Times, 23 December 2001, p. 3.

Gassmann, O. (1997): Internationales F&E-Management – Potentiale und Gestaltungskonzepte transnationaler F&E-Projekte. Oldenbourg: München, Wien.

Gassmann, O. (2001): E-Technologien in dezentralen Innovationsprozessen. Zeitschrift für Betriebswirtschaft, Supplementary Edition 3/2001, pp. 73-90.

Gassmann, O.; von Zedtwitz, M. (1998): Organization of Industrial R&D on a Global Scale. R&D Management, Vol. 28, No. 3, pp. 147-161.

Gassmann, O.; von Zedtwitz, M. (1999): New Concepts and Trends in International R&D Organization. Research Policy, Vol. 28, pp. 231-250.

Gassmann, O.; von Zedtwitz, M. (2003): Trends and Determinants of Managing Virtual R&D Teams. R&D Management, Vol. 33, No. 3, pp. 243-262.

Gassmann, O.; Reepmeyer, G. (2003): Innovationspotentiale im Successful Ageing in der Schweiz. Unpublished report conducted for the Swiss Federal Office for Professional Education and Technology. Bern.

Gassmann, O.; Reepmeyer, G.; von Zedtwitz, M.; (2003): Analyzing Structures of the Pharmaceutical Industry in Switzerland. Journal of Health Care and Society, Vol. 13, No. 2.

Handelszeitung (2002): Pharmamarkt wächst rasant. Handelszeitung, No. 16, 17 April 2002, p. 1.

Hofmann, D. (1997): Das virtuelle Unternehmen. Neue Zürcher Zeitung, 25 October 1997, p. 29.

Hofstede, G. (1980): Culture's Consequences: International Differences in Work Related Values. Beverly Hills.

Homburg & Partner (2001): Trends und Chancen in der Pharma-Branche. Mannheim, April 2001.

Houston, J.G.; Banks, M. (1997): The Chemical-Biological Interface: Developments in Automated and Miniaturised Screening Technology. Current Opinion in Biotechnology, 8, pp. 734-740.

Intercantonal Office for the Control of Medicines (Interkantonale Kontrollstelle für Heilmittel (2002): Public Information, http://www.iks.ch, accessed September 2002.

IHA-IMS (2002): http://www.ihaims.ch, accessed September 2002.

IHA-IMS Health (2002): Taken from Handelszeitung: Pharmamarkt wächst rasant. Handelszeitung, No. 16, 17 April 2002, p. 1.

IMS Health (2000): Pharmaceutical pricing update. Taken from PhRMA (2001): http://www.phrma.org, including information updated in 2001, accessed on 31 March 2003.

Interpharma (2001): Pharma-Markt Schweiz. Ausgabe 2001. Basel.

Jaikumar, R.; Upton, D.M. (1993): The Coordination of Global Manufacturing. In: Bradley, P.; Hausman, J.; Nolan, R. (Eds.): Globalization, Technology, and Competition, Harvard Business School Press: Boston MA.

Jakob, R. (2003): Eines von 47 Biotechunternehmen hat ein erfolgreiches Produkt. New Management, No. 3, pp. 10-13.

KPMG (2002): Pharmaceuticals − Global Insights. By John Morris, Chair of the Europe, Middle East, South Asia, Africa Chemicals & Pharmaceuticals Practice. KPMG Report, February 2002.

Lehman Brothers (1999): Pharmaceutical Outsourcing Digest. 3 December 1999.

Leutenegger, J.-M. (1994): Wettbewerbsorientierte Informationssysteme in der Schweizer Pharma-Branche.

Lichtenberg, F. (1996): The Effect of Pharmaceutical Utilization and Innovation on Hospitalization and Mortality. National Bureau of Economic Research.

Lichtenberg, F. (2000): Are the Benefits of Newer Drugs Worth Their Costs? Evidence from the 1996 MEPS. Health Affairs, 20, 5, p. 241.

Lin, B.-W. (2001): Strategic Alliances and Innovation Networks in the Biopharmaceutical Industry. Institute of Technology Management, National Tsinghua University, Hsinchu, Taiwan.

National Science Board (1996): Science & Engineering Indicators − 1996, NSB 96-21. Washington D.C.: U.S. Government Printing Office.

Nefiodow, L.A. (1990): Der fünfte Kontradieff, Frankfurt.

Nightingale, P. (2000): Economies of Scale in Experimentation: Knowledge and Technology in Pharmaceutical R&D. Industrial and Corporate Change, 9, 2, pp. 315-359.

Nonaka, I.; Takeuchi, H. (1995): The Knowledge-Creating Company. How Japanese Companies Create the Dynamics of Innovation. Oxford: New York.

NZZ (2002): Der Novartis-Hauptsitz bleibt in Basel. Neue Zürcher Zeitung, 16 May 2002, p. 29.

OECD (1999): OECD Health Data. http://www.oecd.org/statistics, accessed September 2002.

OECD (2000): OECD Health Data. http://www.oecd.org/statistics, accessed February 2003.

Pearce, R.D.; Singh, S. (1990): The Internationalisation of Research and Development by Multinational Enterprises: A Firm-level Analysis of Determinants. No. 145, GB-Whiteknights.

Pharma Information (2001): Swiss Health Care and Pharmaceutical Market. Edition 2001. Interpharma: Basel.

Pharma Information (2002): Swiss Health Care and Pharmaceutical Market. Edition 2002. Interpharma: Basel.

Pfeiffer, P. (2000): Sicherung von F&E-Kompetenz in multinationalen Pharmaunternehmen. Dissertation at the University of St. Gallen, Dissertation-No. 2362.

Pfiffner, M.; Stadelmann, P.D. (1995): Arbeit und Management in der Wissensgesellschaft. Dissertation at the University of St. Gallen.

Pfizer (1999): The Pfizer Journal, Vol. 3, Iss. 2, 1999.

PhRMA (2001): http://www.phrma.org, including information updated in 2001, accessed on 31 March 2003.

PhRMA (2002): Pharmaceutical Industry Profile 2002.

PhRMA (2003): Pharmaceutical Research and Manufacturers of America, PhRMA Annual Membership Survey, 2003.

Porter, M. E. (1985): Competitive Advantage: Creating and Sustaining Superior Performance. Macmillan: New York.

Reuters (2002): Pharmaceutical Innovation – An analysis of leading companies and strategies. Reuters Business Insight, Healthcare.

Reuters (2003a): The blockbuster drug outlook to 2007: Identifying, creating and maintaining the pharmaceutical industry's growth drivers. Reuters Business Insight, Healthcare.

Reuters (2003b): Patent Protection Strategies: Maximizing market exclusivity. Reuters Business Insight, Healthcare.

Reuters (2003c): Pharmaceutical R&D Outsourcing Strategies – An analysis of market drivers and resistors to 2010. Reuters Business Insight, Healthcare.

Robbins-Roth, C. (2001): Zukunftsbranche Biotechnologie. Gabler.

Saftlas, H. (2001): Industry Surveys, Healthcare: Pharmaceuticals. Standard & Poors: New York, 27 December 2001, p. 32.

Savioz, P. (2002): Technology Intelligence in Technology-based SMEs – Conceptual Design and Implementation. Zürich.

Schlatter, R. (2002): Pharmamarkt wächst rasant. Handelszeitung, No. 16, 17 April 2002, p. 8.

Shane, S. (1992): Why do some societies invent more than others? Journal of Business Venturing, 7, pp. 29-46.

Shane, S. (1993): Cultural Influences on National Rates of Innovation. Journal of Business Venturing, 8, pp. 59-73.

SSCI (2000): http://www.sgci.ch, accessed September 2002.

SSCI (2002): http://www.sgci.ch, accessed September 2002.

Standort Schweiz (2003): Biotechnology http://www.standortschweiz.ch/seco/internet/en/technologies/biotechnology/index.html, accessed 3 February 2003.

Swissmedic (2002): http://www.swissmedic.ch, accessed September 2002.

Swiss Scientific Council (1999): Fakten & Bewertungen 4/99. In: Pharma Information (2002); based upon Science, Vol. 725, 7 February 1997.

Thurow, L. (1996): The Future of Capitalism. Penguin.

VIPS (2002): Arzneitmittelmarkt Schweiz 2001: Wachstum durch innovative Arzneimittel – VIPS, Pharma Direkt, No. 13, March 2002.

Völker, R. (1999): Wertorientiertes Controlling der Produktentwicklung. Kostenrechnungspraxis, 43, 1999, 4, pp. 201-208.

Völker, R. (2001): Planung und Steuerung von Entwicklungsprojekten in der Pharmabranche. In: Gassmann, O.; Kobe, C.; Voit, E. (Eds.): High-Risk-Projekte. Springer: Berlin, Heidelberg, New York, pp. 231-247.

West, J. (1998): Building a High-Performing Team. In: Cleland, D. (Ed.): Field Guide to Project Management. Wiley: New York, pp. 239-254.

WTO (2002): http://www.wto.org, accessed 18 February 2003.

Wood Mackenzie (2003): As cited in presentation by F. Humer, CEO of Hoffmann-La Roche, June 2003.

von Zedtwitz, M. (1999): Managing Interfaces in International R&D. Dissertation at the University of Gallen, Dissertation-No. 2315.

von Zedtwitz, M.; Gassmann, O. (2002): Market versus Technology Drive in R&D Internationalization: Four Different Patterns of Managing Research and Development. Research Policy, 31, 4, pp. 569-588.

von Zedtwitz, M.; Gassmann, O.; Reepmeyer, G.; (2003): Managing Pharmaceutical R&D – The Case of Switzerland. R&D Management Conference, Manchester, July 2003.

WGZ Bank (2002): Branchenanalyse Life Science. WGZ Report, Oktober 2002. Düsseldorf.

Whittaker, E.; Bower, D. J. (1994): A Shift to External Alliances for Product Development in the Pharmaceutical Industry. R&D Management, Vol. 24, No. 3, pp. 249-260.

Zambrowicz, B.P.; Sands, A.T. (2003): Knockouts Model The 100 Best-Selling Drugs – Will They Model The Next 100? Nature Reviews Drug Discovery, 2, January 2003, pp. 38-51.

Zanetti, P.; Steiner, U. (2001): Sektorstudie Pharma Europa – Biotech als Hoffnungsträger. Leu Investment Research: Zürich.

Zeller, C. (2001): Globalisierungsstrategien – der Weg von Novartis. Springer: Heidelberg.

Index

Glossary

API (Active Pharma-
ceutical Ingredient)
: Any substance or mixture of substances intended to be used in the manufacture of a drug. When used in the production of a drug, it becomes an active ingredient of the drug product.

Biochips
: While containing DNA, Biochips are used to automate the sequencing of genes.

Bioinformatics
: The use of IT in pharmaceutical R&D (e.g., electronic databases of genomes and protein sequences, and computer modeling of biomolecules and biologic systems). Bioinformatics is expected to expedite lead discovery by providing structural data and analysis for drug targets.

Bioprocessing
: The creation of a product utilizing a living organism.

Blockbuster
: A pharmaceutical product earning annual revenues in excess of US$ 1 billion.

Chemoinformatics
: The combination of chemical synthesis, biological screening, and data mining approaches used to guide drug discovery and development.

Cloning
: Using specialized DNA technology to produce multiple, exact copies of a single gene or other segment of DNA. The resulting, cloned (copied) collections of DNA molecules are also referred to as clone libraries. A second type of cloning exploits the natural process of cell division to make many copies of an entire cell. The genetic makeup of these cloned cells, called a cell line, is identical to the original cell. A third type of cloning pro-

duces complete, genetically identical organisms (e.g., animals).

Combinatorial Chemistry	It allows large numbers of compounds to be made by the systemic and repetitive covalent connection of a set of different 'building blocks' of varying structures to each other.
Compounding	Bringing together excipient and solvent components into a homogeneous mix of active ingredients.
CSO (Contract Service Organization)	Any organization that provides pharmaceutical companies with a contract service. Among others, the term CSO includes: CROs (contract research organizations), CMOs (contract manufacturing organizations), SMOs (site management organizations).
Diagnostic	A substance or group of substances used to identify a disease by analyzing cause and symptoms.
DNA (Deoxyribonucleic Acid)	DNA represents the molecular basis for genes. Every inherited characteristic has its origin somewhere in the code of an organism's complement of DNA.
Efficacy	The ability of a substance to produce a desired effect.
Enzyme	Macromolecules, mostly of protein nature, that function as (bio-) catalysts. They not only promote reactions but also function as regulators making sure the organism does not produce too much or too little of any chemical substance.
FDA	Food and Drug Administration (US regulatory approval body for new pharmaceutical products).
Gene	A natural unit of hereditary material that is the physical basis for the transmission of the charac-

teristics of living organisms from one generation to another. The basic genetic material is essentially the same in all living organisms. It consists of deoxyribonucleic acid (DNA) in most organisms and ribonucleic acid (RNA) in certain viruses.

Gene Mapping
Determination of the relative positions of genes on a DNA molecule (chromosome or plasmid) and of the distance (in linkage units or physical units) between them.

Gene Sequencing
The determination of the sequence of bases in a DNA strand.

Gene Splicing
The enzymatic attachment of one gene or part of a gene to another.

Generic Drug
Replication of a prescription or non-prescription drug where the patent protection has expired. Generic drugs (also referred to as generics) are usually offered by firms that did not develop the drugs themselves but gained a license to sell the drug.

Genetics
The study of the genetic composition, heredity, and variation of organisms.

Genetic Diseases
Diseases that occur because of a mutation in the genetic material.

Genetic Engineering
The selective, deliberate alteration of genes by technological means.

Genomics
The process of identifying genes involved in disease through the comparison of the genomes of individuals with and without disease.

Genomic Library
A collection of clones made from a set of randomly generated overlapping DNA fragments representing the entire genome of an organism.

High-throughput Screening	The process for the rapid assessment of the activity of samples from a combinatorial library or other compound collection.
Immunology	The study of how the body defends itself against disease.
IND (Investigational New Drug) Application	A document filed with the FDA prior to clinical trial of a new drug. It gives a full description of the new drug, such as where and how it is manufactured. An IND permission has to be kept active annually by sending, for example, annual reports. The IND is followed by the NDA (New Drug Application).
Molecular Genetics	The study of the nature and biochemistry of genetic material. It includes the technologies of genetic engineering.
NCE (New Chemical Entity)	Referring to newly approved pharmaceutical products.
NDA (New Drug Application)	The process of determining the benefit-risk profile of a new drug after completion of the clinical tests and prior to approval for marketing.
NME (New Molecular Entity)	Referring to newly approved pharmaceutical products.
Orphan Drug	A drug that is believed to substantially increase the life expectancy of the treated patient for a particular disease. While developing an orphan drug, competitors are usually excluded from receiving a license to produce a similar drug for a finite period (usually 7 years), thereby allowing the company producing the drug to recuperate R&D expenses.
OTC (Over-the-Counter) Drug	A drug that can usually be purchased without a prescription. An OTC drug is also sometimes re-

ferred to as a drug purely used for self-medication purposes and is typically used for minor ailments such as headache or the flu.

Pharmacodynamics	Quantitative study of drug action.
Pharmacogenomics	The study of how the response to a drug is affected by individual genetic variations. It is aimed at the prescription or development of drugs that maximize benefit and minimize side effects in individuals.
Pharmacokinetics	Quantitative study of how drugs are taken up, biologically transformed, distributed, metabolized, and eliminated from the body.
PhRMA	Pharmaceutical Research and Manufacturers of America (an organization representing the leading research-based pharmaceutical and biotechnology companies in the US).
Proteomics	The study of the entire protein output of cells. It refers to any protein-based approach that has the capacity to provide new information about proteins on a genome-wide scale.
RNA (Ribonucleic Acid)	A single-strand molecule that partners with DNA to manufacture proteins.
Recombinant	Recombining of generic material from one species into alternate sequences.
Target	The target molecule is usually responsible for causing a respective disease. The targets of most drugs are proteins. The drug molecule, which is supposed to cure the respective disease, inserts itself into a functionally important crevice of the target protein, like a key in a lock. The drug molecule is then connected to the target and either induces or, more commonly, inhibits the protein's normal function.

Toxicogenomics	Application of genetic and genomic methods to the study of toxicology.
Toxicology	Study of poisonous substances in terms of their chemistry, effects, and treatments.
Treatment Investigational New Drug	An Investigational New Drug that makes a promising new drug available to desperately ill patients as early in the drug development process as available. The FDA permits the drug to be used if there is preliminary evidence of efficacy and it treats a serious or life-threatening disease, or if there is no comparable therapy available.
Vaccine	An agent containing antigens. It is used for stimulating the immune system of the recipient to produce specific antibodies providing active immunity and/or passive immunity in the progeny.

Authors

Prof. Dr. Oliver Gassmann is Professor of Technology Management and Director of the Institute of Technology Management at the University of St. Gallen, Switzerland. Prior to joining the Institute of Technology Management in St. Gallen, Oliver Gassmann was Vice President of Technology Management at Schindler in Ebikon, Switzerland. While at Schindler, he was the Head of Corporate Research and Advanced Development worldwide. During his tenure, he worked on multiple international projects across Europe and Asia.

Oliver Gassmann holds a master's degree in business and economics from the University of Hohenheim, Germany, and received a Ph.D. with highest distinction from the University of St. Gallen, Switzerland. He is a member of several scientific and economic boards, including the editorial boards of R&D Management and the International Journal of Entrepreneurship and Innovation Management as well as the Research Committee of the University of St. Gallen. In addition, he is a member of the national committee for science and research (Economiesuisse) and won the 1998 RADMA prize. He published six books and more than 80 articles in leading international journals in the area of technology and innovation management.

Gerrit Reepmeyer is Research Associate at the Institute of Technology Management at the University of St. Gallen, Switzerland. Before joining the Institute of Technology Management in St. Gallen, he worked in the position of a Manager with the venture capital firm KnowledgeCube Group, Inc. in New York. Gerrit Reepmeyer holds a master's degree in business & engineering from Technical University Berlin, Germany, as well as an MS in Management from Stevens Institute of Technology in cooperation with New York University, USA. While studying in the US, he was a scholar of the German Academic Exchange Service (DAAD).

Gerrit Reepmeyer focuses his research on R&D management with an emphasis on the pharmaceutical industry. He has published articles on pharmaceutical R&D as well as the impact of demographics on innovation management. He also contributed a chapter in a book on corporate finance management.

Prof. Dr. Maximilian von Zedtwitz is Associate Professor of Technology & Innovation Management at Tsinghua University, Beijing, P.R. China. Before that, he was a Professor of Technology Management at IMD, Lausanne, Switzerland, and a Visiting Fellow at Harvard University, Cambridge, Massachusetts. He has a Ph.D. in Technology Management and a lic. oec. (MBA) degree from the University of St. Gallen, as well as M.Sc. and B.Sc. degrees in Computer Science from ETH-Zurich (Swiss Federal Institute of Technology). He minored in Japanese studies at the University of Zurich.

Max von Zedtwitz teaches international innovation strategy, R&D management, and technology-based incubation in MBA, Ph.D., and executive education programs. Having published more than 40 articles in leading practitioner and academic journals and four books, he has won several awards for research excellence and publications. He serves on the editorial boards of R&D Management and four other international journals reporting research on innovation, entrepreneurship, and technology management.